NEW!

LOOK FOR THE CAMERA in our in
technique videos made just for you! **www**

MW00667256

99 Snowflakes
Volume 2

LEISURE ARTS, INC. • Maumelle, Arkansas

EDITORIAL STAFF

Vice President of Editorial: Susan White Sullivan
Creative Art Director: Katherine Laughlin
Publications Director: Leah Lampirez
Special Projects Director: Susan Frantz Wiles
Technical Writers: Linda A. Daley and Cathy Hardy
Technical Editors: Sarah J. Green and Lois J. Long
Art Category Manager: Lora Puls
Graphic Artists: Kara Darling, Lora Puls and Becca Snider Tally
Prepress Technician: Stephanie Johnson
Contributing Photographer: Mark Mathews
Contributing Photo Stylist: Christy Myers

BUSINESS STAFF

President and Chief Executive Officer: Rick Barton
Senior Vice President of Operations: Jim Dittrich
Vice President of Finance: Fred F. Pruss
Vice President of Sales-Retail Books: Martha Adams
Vice President of Mass Market: Bob Bewighouse
Vice President of Technology and Planning: Laticia Mull Dittrich
Controller: Tiffany P. Childers
Information Technology Director: Brian Roden
Director of E-Commerce Services: Mark Hawkins
Manager of E-Commerce: Robert Young
Retail Customer Service Manager: Stan Raynor

Made in China

Library of Congress Control Number: 2013948964

ISBN-13: 978-1-4647-0401-7

Adorn your holiday tree and home with a flurry of snowflakes!

These 99 thread crochet designs by Terese Poehnelt can be used as tree ornaments or to decorate windows, gifts, and more. The patterns are organized by skill levels from Easy+ to Intermediate, and free online videos are available to help with basic and special techniques. Snowflake collectors will love that each pattern is different and unique! Blocking diagrams and starching instructions are included.

Let it snow,
let it snow,
let it snow!

Contents

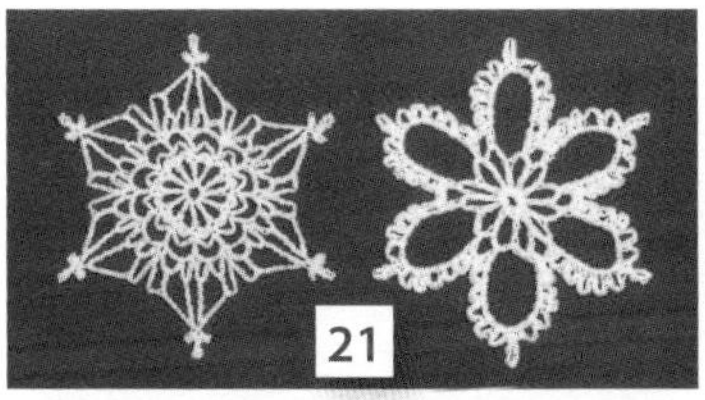
21
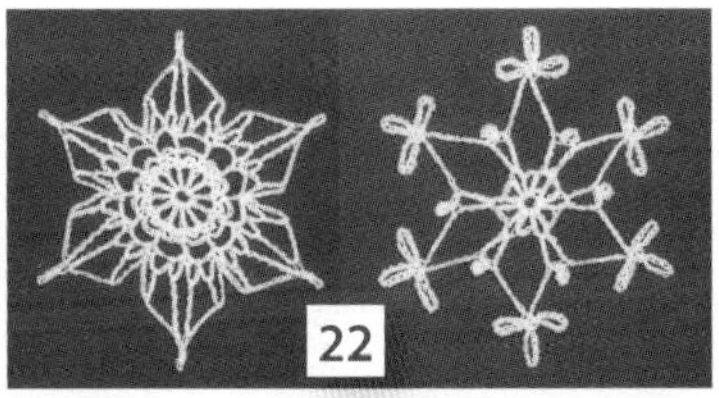
22
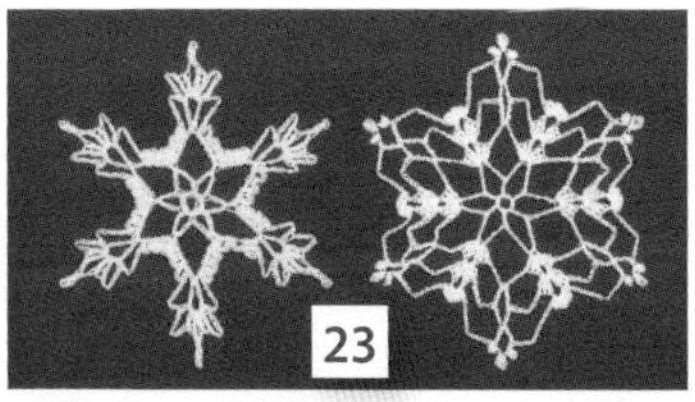
23
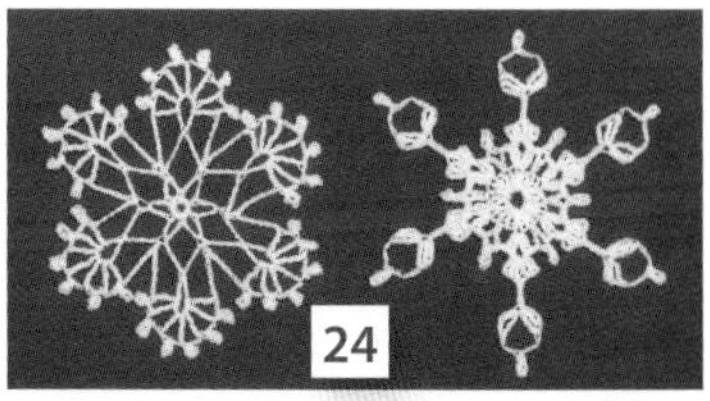
24
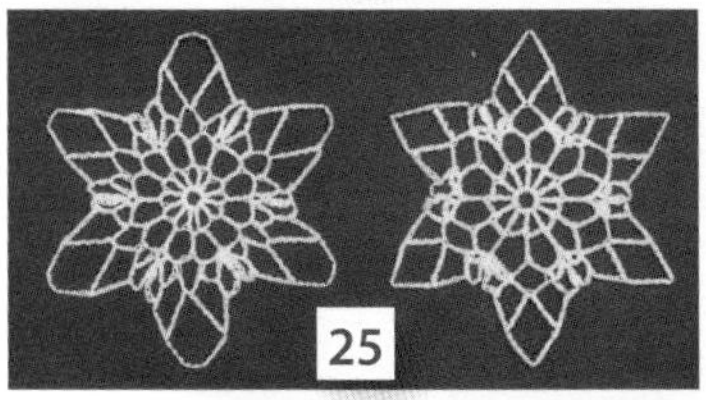
25
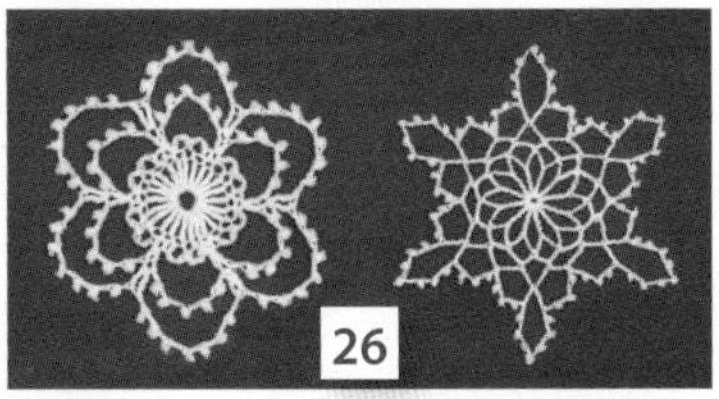
26
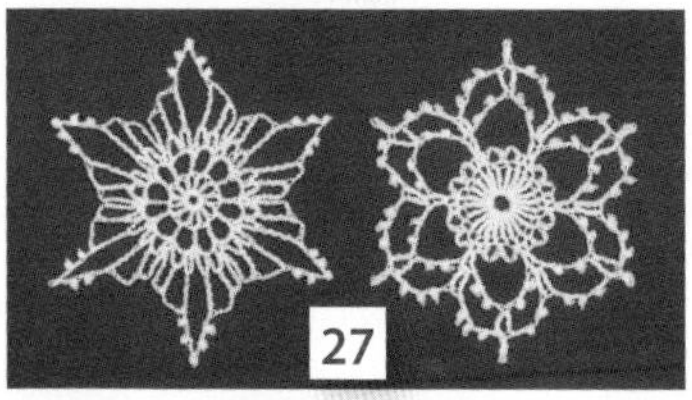
27
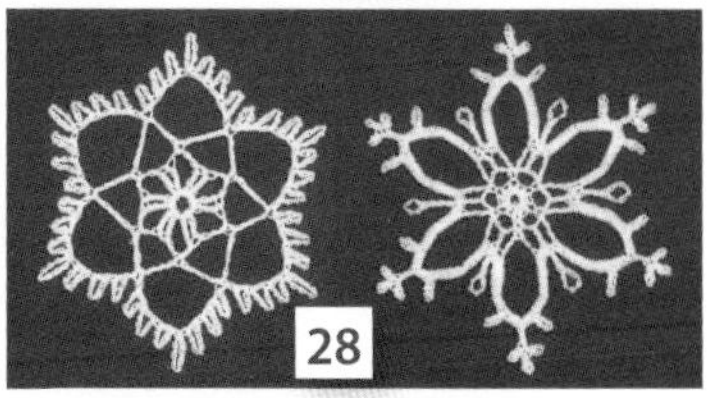
28
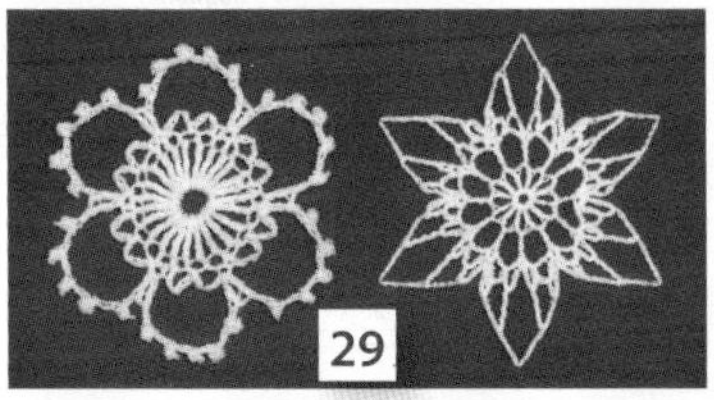
29
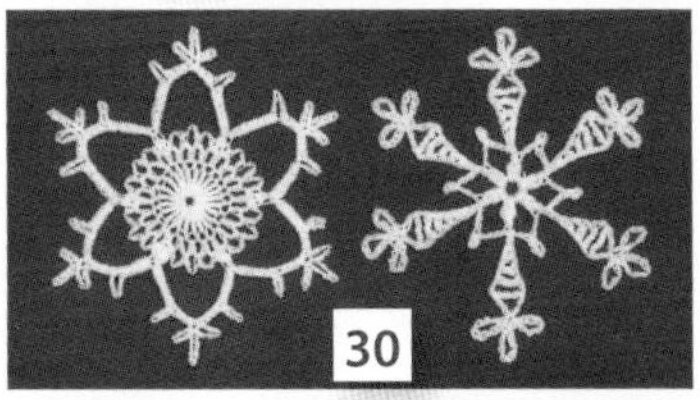
30
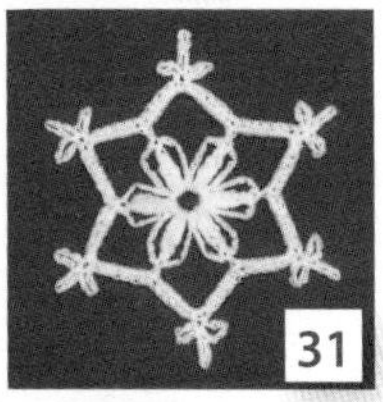
31

32

33

34

35
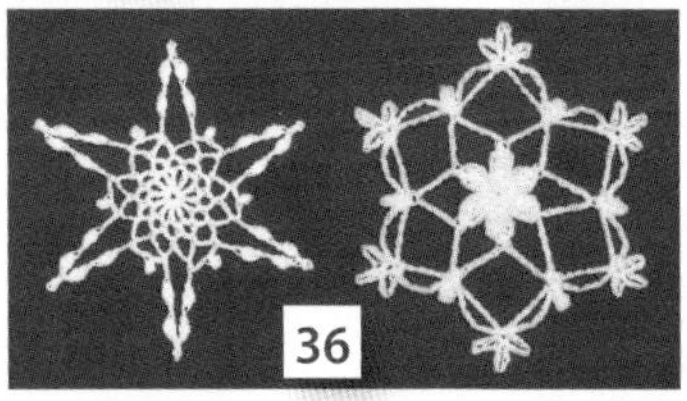
36

37
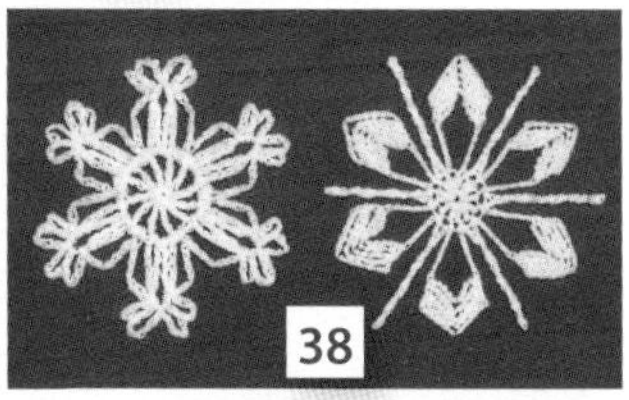
38
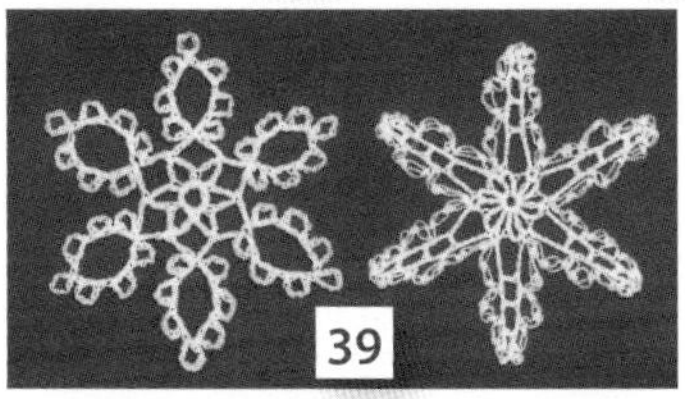
39
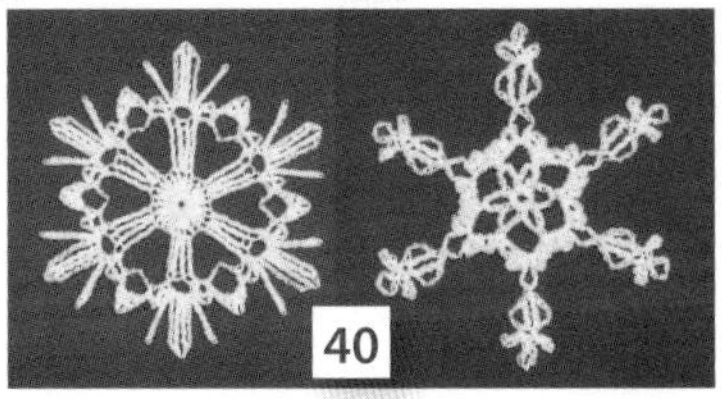
40
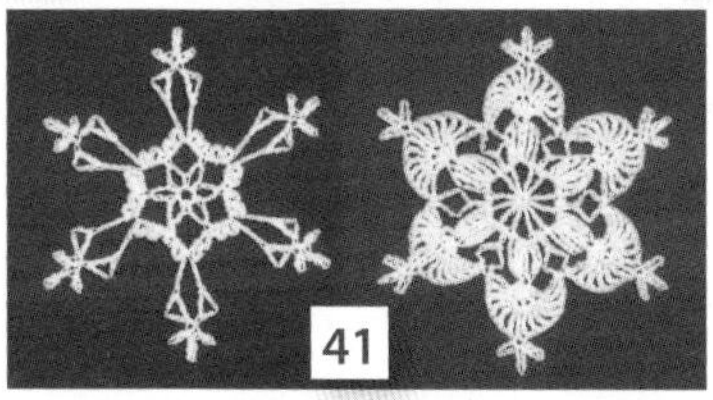
41
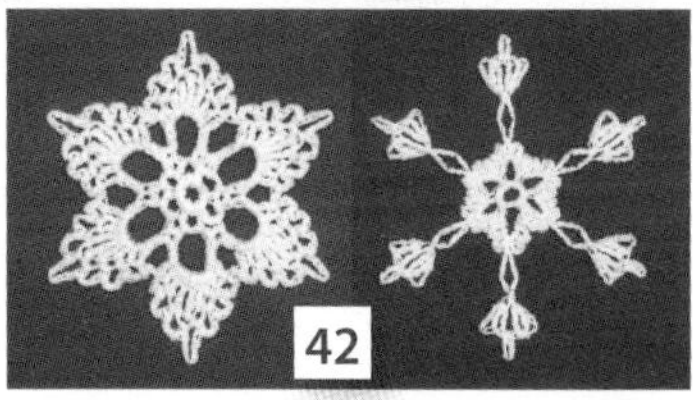
42
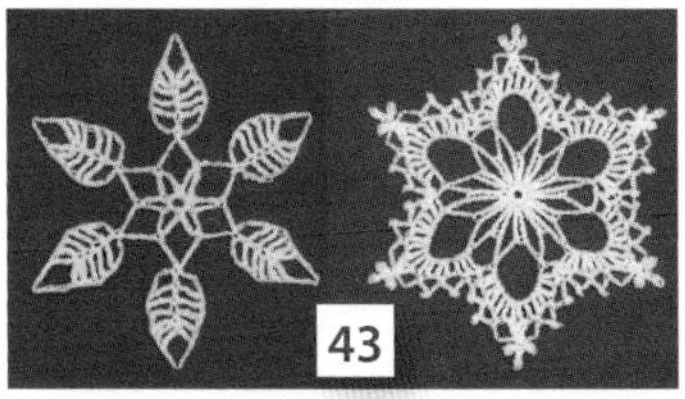
43

44
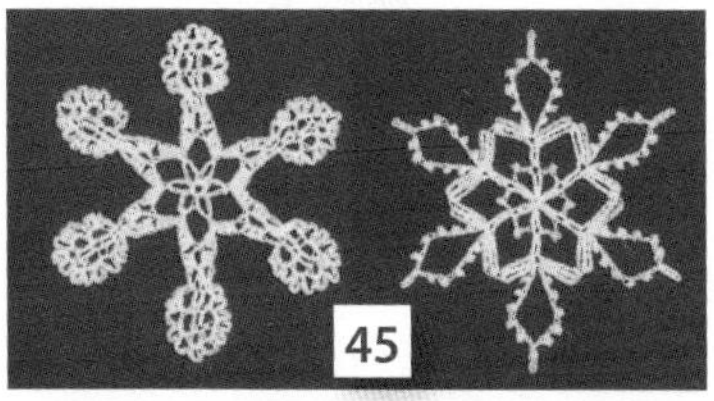
45
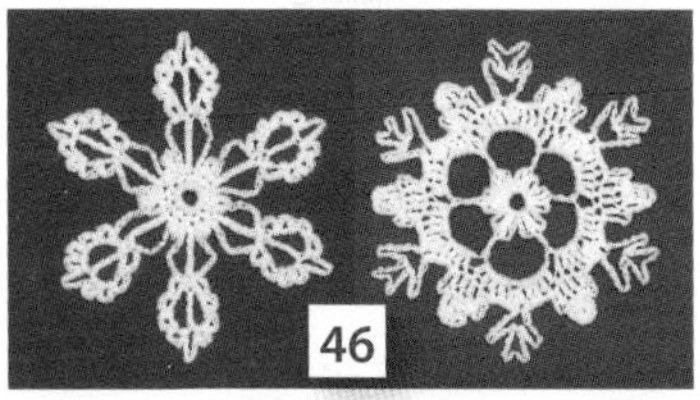
46
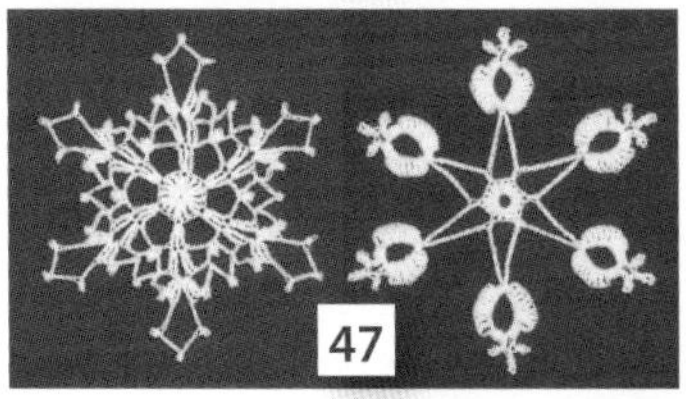
47
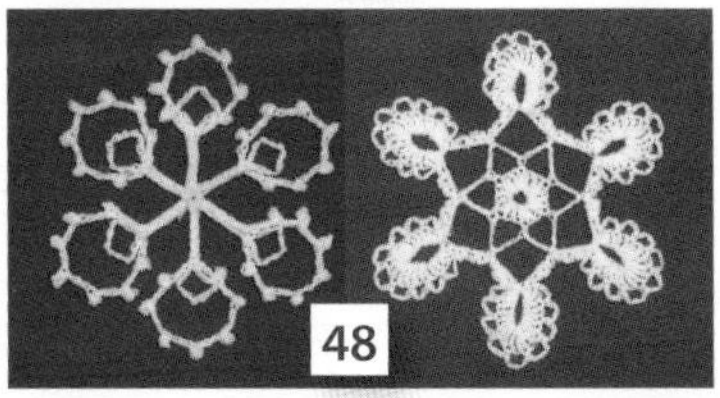
48
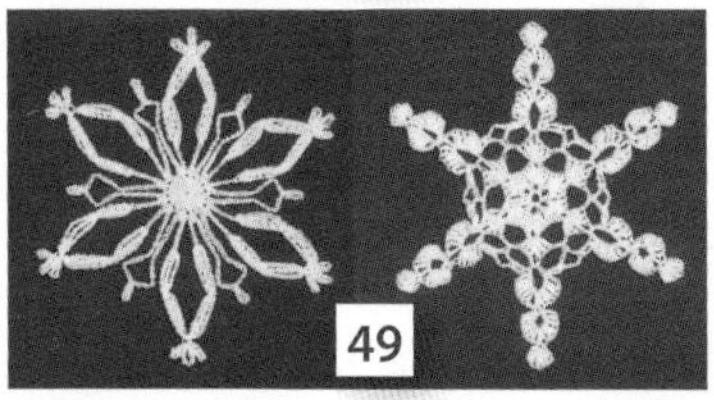
49
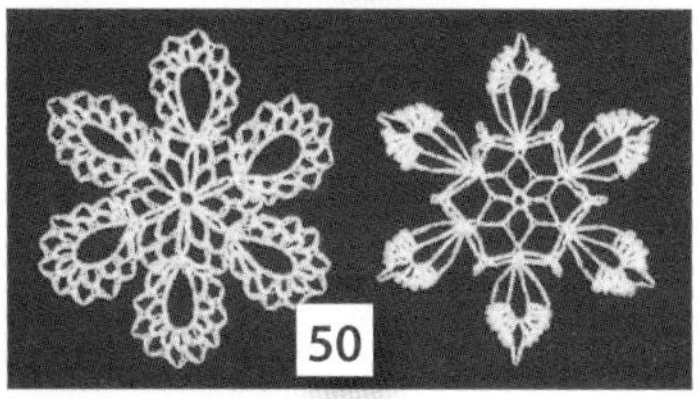
50
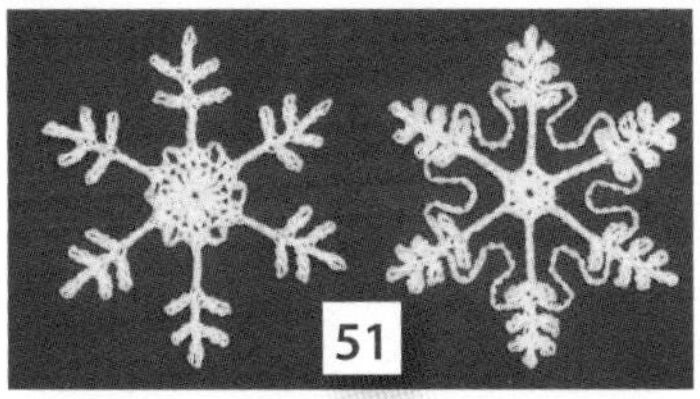
51
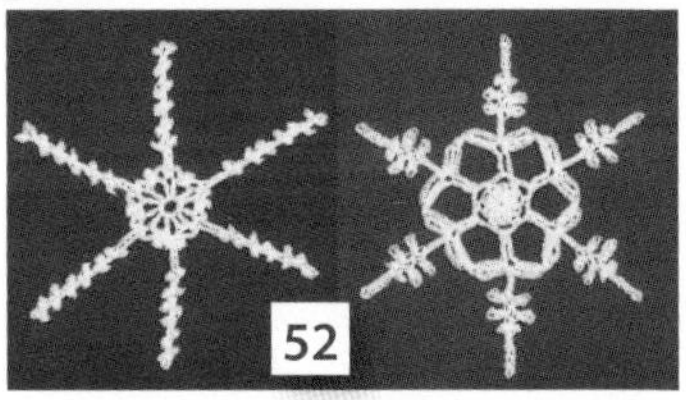
52
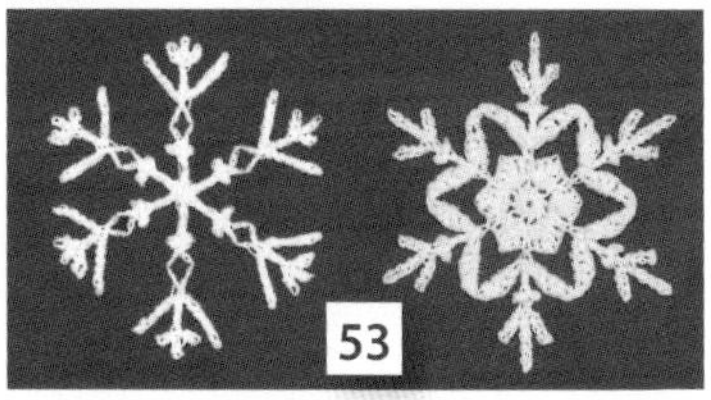
53

54

55
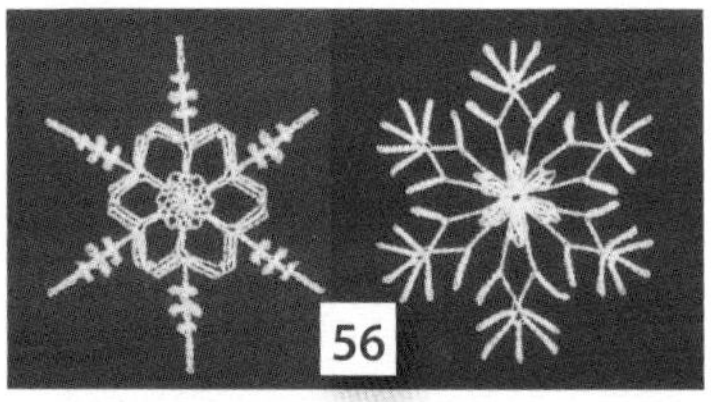
56

SHOPPING LIST

Thread (Lace Weight)

Crochet thread, size 10

LACE 0

5-30 yards (4.5-27.5 meters) for **each** Snowflake, depending on the size and complexity

Crochet Hook

- ☐ Size 6 (1.8 mm)

Starching Supplies

- ☐ Terry towel
- ☐ Fabric stiffener
- ☐ Resealable plastic bag
- ☐ Tracing paper
- ☐ Waterproof marking pen
- ☐ Blocking board
- ☐ Plastic wrap
- ☐ Paper towels
- ☐ Rust-proof straight pins
- ☐ Acrylic spray (optional)

Additional Supplies

- ☐ Translucent nylon thread

Finished Sizes: Approximate sizes **after** starching are listed with the individual instructions.

The instructions in this leaflet are written for bedspread weight cotton thread (size 10). Gauge is not of great importance; your Snowflakes may be a bit larger or smaller without changing the overall effect.

1

EASY +

Finished Size: Approximately $2\frac{3}{4}$" (7 cm) diameter

INSTRUCTIONS

Ch 4; join with slip st to form a ring.

Rnd 1 (Right side)**:** Ch 8, (dc in ring, ch 5) 5 times; join with slip st to 3rd ch of beginning ch-8: 6 ch-5 sps.

Rnd 2: (Slip st, ch 1, sc) in next ch-5 sp, ★ † (ch 3, sc in same sp) twice, ch 10, slip st in 5th ch from hook, ch 5 †, sc in next ch-5 sp; repeat from ★ 4 times **more**, then repeat from † to † once; join with slip st to first sc, finish off.

See Starching, page 61. Use 6-Point Blocking Pattern, page 62.

2

EASY +

Finished Size: Approximately $4\frac{3}{4}$" (12 cm) diameter

INSTRUCTIONS

Ch 6; join with slip st to form a ring.

Rnd 1 (Right side)**:** Ch 1, sc in ring, ★ † ch 6, slip st in 5th ch from hook, ch 1, sc in ring, ch 10, slip st in 4th ch from hook, ch 20, slip st in 17th ch from hook, ch 7, slip st in 4th ch from hook, ch 6 †, sc in ring; repeat from ★ 4 times **more**, then repeat from † to † once; join with slip st to first sc, finish off.

See Starching, page 61. Use 6-Point Blocking Pattern, page 62.

3

EASY +

Finished Size: Approximately 4" (10 cm) diameter

INSTRUCTIONS

Ch 5; join with slip st to form a ring.

Rnd 1 (Right side)**:** Ch 2 **(counts as first hdc)**, 17 hdc in ring; join with slip st to first hdc: 18 hdc.

Rnd 2: ★ Ch 6, slip st in 3rd ch from hook, (ch 3, slip st in 3rd ch from hook) 14 times, ch 3, slip st in same st on Rnd 1 as last st worked into, ch 6, slip st in 3rd ch from hook, ch 3, skip next 2 hdc, slip st in next hdc; repeat from ★ around working last slip st in joining slip st, finish off.

See Starching, page 61. Use 12-Point Blocking Pattern, page 63.

4

EASY +

Finished Size: Approximately 3 1/2" (9 cm) diameter

INSTRUCTIONS

Ch 6; join with slip st to form a ring.

Rnd 1 (Right side)**:** Ch 5 **(counts as first dc plus ch 2)**, (dc in ring, ch 2) 11 times; join with slip st to first dc: 12 dc and 12 ch-2 sps.

Rnd 2: Ch 1, sc in same st as joining, ★ † [ch 12, slip st in 6th ch from hook, (ch 7, slip st in 6th ch from hook) twice **(3-Picot group made)**], slip st in ch at base of first Picot, ch 6, sc in next dc, ch 12, slip st in 6th ch from hook, ch 6 †, sc in next dc; repeat from ★ 4 times **more**, then repeat from † to † once; join with slip st to first sc, finish off.

See Starching, page 61. Use 12-Point Blocking Pattern, page 63.

5

EASY +

Finished Size: Approximately 4" (10 cm) diameter

INSTRUCTIONS

Rnd 1 (Right side)**:** Ch 3, 11 hdc in 3rd ch from hook; join with slip st in top of beginning ch-3: 12 sts.

Rnd 2: Ch 8, skip next hdc, dc in next hdc, ★ ch 5, skip next hdc, dc in next hdc; repeat from ★ around to last hdc, ch 2, skip last hdc, dc in 3rd ch of beginning ch-8 to form last ch-5 sp: 6 ch-5 sps.

Rnd 3: Ch 1, sc in last ch-5 sp made, ★ † ch 9, hdc in 4th ch from hook, (ch 4, hdc in 4th ch from hook) twice, ch 6, slip st in 6th ch from hook, (ch 4, hdc in 4th ch from hook) 3 times, slip st in ch at base of first hdc to form a loop, ch 5 †, sc in next ch-5 sp; repeat from ★ 4 times **more**, then repeat from † to † once; join with slip st to first sc, finish off.

See Starching, page 61. Use 6-Point Blocking Pattern, page 62.

EASY +

Finished Size: Approximately 3 1/4" (8.5 cm) diameter

INSTRUCTIONS

Ch 6; join with slip st to form a ring.

Rnd 1 (Right side)**:** Ch 1, sc in ring, (ch 5, sc in ring) 5 times, ch 2, dc in first sc to form last ch-5 sp: 6 ch-5 sps.

Rnd 2: Ch 1, sc in last ch-5 sp made, ch 13, slip st in 9th ch from hook to form a ring, ch 4, ★ sc in next ch-5 sp, ch 13, slip st in 9th ch from hook, ch 4; repeat from ★ around; join with slip st to first sc: 6 sc, 6 rings, and 12 ch-4 sps.

Rnd 3: Ch 1, sc in same st as joining, ★ † ch 5, sc in next ch-4 sp, ch 7, dc in next ring, ch 6, slip st in top of last dc made ***(Fig. 1a, page 58)***, ch 7, sc in next ch-4 sp, ch 5 †, sc in next sc; repeat from ★ 4 times **more**, then repeat from † to † once; join with slip st to first sc, finish off.

See Starching, page 61. Use 6-Point Blocking Pattern, page 62.

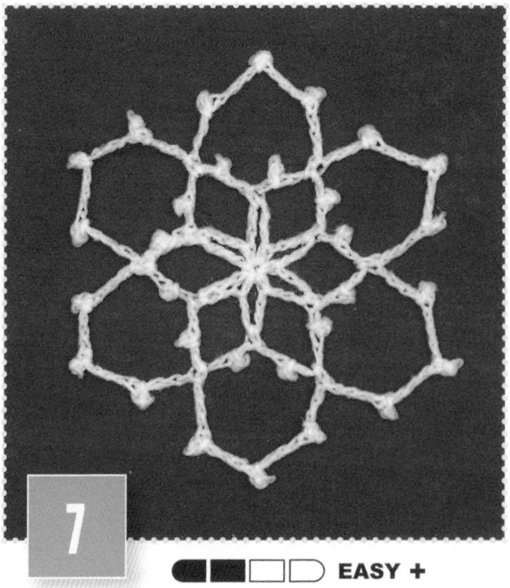

EASY +

Finished Size: Approximately 3 1/4" (8.5 cm) diameter

INSTRUCTIONS

Ch 5; join with slip st to form a ring.

Rnd 1 (Right side)**:** Ch 1, sc in ring, (ch 6, sc in ring) 5 times, ch 3, dc in first sc to form last ch-6 sp: 6 ch-6 sps.

Rnd 2: Ch 1, sc in last ch-6 sp made, ch 4, slip st in 3rd ch from hook, ch 6, slip st in 3rd ch from hook, ch 1, ★ sc in next ch-6 sp, ch 4, slip st in 3rd ch from hook, ch 6, slip st in 3rd ch from hook, ch 1; repeat from ★ around; join with slip st to first sc: 6 loops.

Rnd 3: Slip st across to center ch of next loop, ch 1, sc in same loop, (ch 6, slip st in 3rd ch from hook) 3 times, ch 3, ★ sc in center ch of next loop, (ch 6, slip st in 3rd ch from hook) 3 times, ch 3; repeat from ★ around; join with slip st to first sc, finish off.

See Starching, page 61. Use 6-Point Blocking Pattern, page 62.

EASY +

Finished Size: Approximately 2" (5 cm) diameter

INSTRUCTIONS

Ch 5; join with slip st to form a ring.

Rnd 1 (Right side)**:** Ch 3 **(counts as first dc)**, dc in ring, ch 5, (2 dc in ring, ch 5) 5 times; join with slip st to first dc: 12 dc and 6 ch-5 sps.

Rnd 2: Slip st in next dc, ch 1, sc in same st, (3 dc, ch 5, 3 dc) in next ch-5 sp, ★ skip next dc, sc in next dc, (3 dc, ch 5, 3 dc) in next ch-5 sp; repeat from ★ around to last st, skip last st; join with slip st to first sc, finish off.

See Starching, page 61. Use 6-Point Blocking Pattern, page 62.

9

EASY +

Finished Size: Approximately 3" (7.5 cm) diameter

This snowflake begins the same as #8. Add one more round for a slightly larger snowflake with a different look.

INSTRUCTIONS

Ch 5; join with slip st to form a ring.

Rnd 1 (Right side)**:** Ch 3 **(counts as first dc)**, dc in ring, ch 5, (2 dc in ring, ch 5) 5 times; join with slip st to first dc: 12 dc and 6 ch-5 sps.

Rnd 2: Slip st in next dc, ch 1, sc in same st, (3 dc, ch 5, 3 dc) in next ch-5 sp, ★ skip next dc, sc in next dc, (3 dc, ch 5, 3 dc) in next ch-5 sp; repeat from ★ around to last st, skip last st; join with slip st to first sc: 42 sts and 6 ch-5 sps.

Rnd 3: Ch 5, ★ † (dc, ch 2, dc, ch 7, dc, ch 2, dc) in next ch-5 sp, ch 3, skip next 3 dc †, hdc in next sc, ch 3; repeat from ★ 4 times **more**, then repeat from † to † once; join with slip st to 2nd ch of beginning ch-5, finish off.

See Starching, page 61. Use 6-Point Blocking Pattern, page 62.

10

EASY +

Finished Size: Approximately 4" (10 cm) diameter

This snowflake begins the same as #8 and #9. Add the same round as #9, then one more for an even larger snowflake, changing the look again.

INSTRUCTIONS

Ch 5; join with slip st to form a ring.

Rnd 1 (Right side)**:** Ch 3 **(counts as first dc)**, dc in ring, ch 5, (2 dc in ring, ch 5) 5 times; join with slip st to first dc: 12 dc and 6 ch-5 sps.

Rnd 2: Slip st in next dc, ch 1, sc in same st, (3 dc, ch 5, 3 dc) in next ch-5 sp, ★ skip next dc, sc in next dc, (3 dc, ch 5, 3 dc) in next ch-5 sp; repeat from ★ around to last st, skip last st; join with slip st to first sc: 42 sts and 6 ch-5 sps.

Rnd 3: Ch 5, ★ † (dc, ch 2, dc, ch 7, dc, ch 2, dc) in next ch-5 sp, ch 3, skip next 3 dc †, hdc in next sc, ch 3; repeat from ★ 4 times **more**, then repeat from † to † once; join with slip st to 2nd ch of beginning ch-5: 30 sts and 30 sps.

Rnd 4: Ch 4, ★ † (dc in next dc, ch 2) twice, (3 dc, ch 2) twice in next ch-7 sp, (dc in next dc, ch 2) twice †, hdc in next hdc, ch 2; repeat from ★ 4 times **more**, then repeat from † to † once; join with slip st to 2nd ch of beginning ch-4, finish off.

See Starching, page 61. Use 6-Point Blocking Pattern, page 62.

11

EASY +

Finished Size: Approximately $4^{1}/_{4}$" (11 cm) diameter

INSTRUCTIONS

Ch 6; join with slip st to form a ring.

Rnd 1 (Right side)**:** Ch 1, sc in ring, (ch 5, sc in ring) 5 times, ch 2, dc in first sc to form last ch-5 sp: 6 ch-5 sps.

Rnd 2: Ch 1, sc in last ch-5 sp made, ch 13, slip st in 9th ch from hook to form a ring, ch 4, ★ sc in next ch-5 sp, ch 13, slip st in 9th ch from hook, ch 4; repeat from ★ around; join with slip st to first sc: 6 rings and 12 ch-4 sps.

Rnd 3: (Slip st, ch 1, sc) in next ch-4 sp, ★ † (ch 3, sc in same sp) twice, ch 2, dc in next ring, ch 4, slip st in 4th ch from hook, (ch 5, slip st in 4th ch from hook, dc in same ring) 6 times, ch 2, sc in next ch-4 sp, (ch 3, sc in same sp) twice †, sc in next ch-4 sp; repeat from ★ 4 times **more**, then repeat from † to † once; join with slip st to first sc, finish off.

See Starching, page 61. Use 6-Point Blocking Pattern, page 62.

12

EASY +

Finished Size: Approximately $4^{3}/_{4}$" (12 cm) diameter

INSTRUCTIONS

Ch 6; join with slip st to form a ring.

Rnd 1 (Right side)**:** Ch 3 **(counts as first dc)**, dc in ring, (ch 5, 2 dc in ring) 5 times, ch 2, dc in first dc to form last ch-5 sp: 6 ch-5 sps.

Rnd 2: Ch 1, sc in last ch-5 sp made, ch 13, slip st in 9th ch from hook to form a ring, ch 4, ★ sc in next ch-5 sp, ch 13, slip st in 9th ch from hook, ch 4; repeat from ★ around; join with slip st to first sc: 6 rings and 12 ch-4 sps.

Rnd 3: (Slip st, ch 1, sc) in next ch-4 sp, ★ † (ch 3, sc in same sp) 3 times, ch 5, (sc, ch 5, 2 dc) in next ring, ch 6, slip st in 5th ch from hook, ch 1, (2 dc, ch 5, sc) in same ring, ch 5, sc in next ch-4 sp, (ch 3, sc in same sp) 3 times †, sc in next ch-4 sp; repeat from ★ 4 times **more**, then repeat from † to † once; join with slip st to first sc, finish off.

See Starching, page 61. Use 6-Point Blocking Pattern, page 62.

13

EASY +

Finished Size: Approximately $3^{3}/_{4}$" (9.5 cm) diameter

INSTRUCTIONS

Rnd 1 (Right side)**:** Ch 8, (dc, ch 4) 5 times in 8th ch from hook; join with slip st to 4th ch of beginning ch-8: 6 sts and 6 ch-4 sps.

Rnd 2: Ch 15, slip st in same st as joining, ★ ch 6, (slip st, ch 15, slip st) in next dc; repeat from ★ around, ch 3, dc in joining slip st to form last ch-6 sp: 6 ch-6 sps and 6 loops.

Rnd 3: Ch 1, sc in last ch-6 sp made, ★ † ch 2, sc in next loop, (ch 3, sc in same loop) twice, ch 7, slip st in top of last sc made ***(Fig. 1a, page 58)***, (ch 3, sc in same loop) twice, ch 2 †, sc in next ch-6 sp; repeat from ★ 4 times **more**, then repeat from † to † once; join with slip st to first sc, finish off.

See Starching, page 61. Use 6-Point Blocking Pattern, page 62.

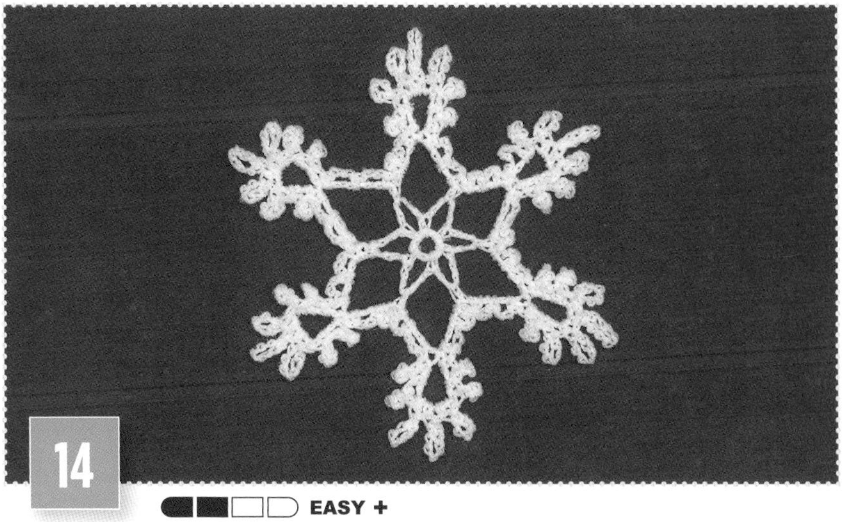

14

EASY +

Finished Size: Approximately 4" (10 cm) diameter

INSTRUCTIONS

Ch 6; join with slip st to form a ring.

Rnd 1 (Right side)**:** Ch 1, sc in ring, (ch 5, sc in ring) 5 times, ch 2, dc in first sc to form last ch-5 sp: 6 ch-5 sps.

Rnd 2: Ch 1, sc in last ch-5 sp made, ch 13, slip st in 9th ch from hook to form a ring, ch 4, ★ sc in next ch-5 sp, ch 13, slip st in 9th ch from hook, ch 4; repeat from ★ around; join with slip st to first sc: 6 rings and 12 ch-4 sps.

Rnd 3: (Slip st, ch 1, sc) in next ch-4 sp, ★ † (ch 3, sc in same sp) twice, sc in next ring, ch 5, slip st in 5th ch from hook, sc in same ring, ch 6, slip st in 6th ch from hook, sc in same ring, ch 7, slip st in 7th ch from hook, sc in same ring, ch 8, slip st in 8th ch from hook, sc in same ring, ch 7, slip st in 7th ch from hook, sc in same ring, ch 6, slip st in 6th ch from hook, sc in same ring, ch 5, slip st in 5th ch from hook, sc in same ring and in next ch-4 sp, (ch 3, sc in same sp) twice †, sc in next ch-4 sp; repeat from ★ 4 times **more**, then repeat from † to † once; join with slip st to first sc, finish off.

See Starching, page 61. Use 6-Point Blocking Pattern, page 62.

15

EASY +

Finished Size: Approximately 4" (10 cm) diameter

INSTRUCTIONS

Ch 12; join with slip st to form a ring.

Rnd 1 (Right side)**:** Ch 1, sc in same ch as joining, ★ † ch 10, dc in 7th ch from hook, **[**ch 15, slip st in 6th ch from hook, ch 7, slip st in 7th ch from hook, ch 6, slip st in 6th ch from hook **(3-Picot group made)]**, slip st in ch at base of first Picot, ch 9, (slip st, ch 6, dc) in top of last dc made *(Fig. 1a, page 58)*, ch 3, skip next ch of ring †, sc in next ch; repeat from ★ 4 times **more**, then repeat from † to † once; join with slip st to first sc, finish off.

See Starching, page 61. Use 6-Point Blocking Pattern, page 62.

16

EASY +

Finished Size: Approximately 5" (12.5 cm) diameter

INSTRUCTIONS

Ch 5; join with slip st to form a ring.

Rnd 1 (Right side)**:** Ch 1, 12 sc in ring; join with slip st to first sc.

Rnd 2: Ch 1, sc in same st as joining, ch 3, (sc in next sc, ch 3) around; join with slip st to first sc: 12 ch-3 sps.

Rnd 3: Slip st in next ch-3 sp, ch 1, (sc, ch 9, sc) in same sp, ch 3, sc in next ch-3 sp, ch 3, ★ (sc, ch 9, sc) in next ch-3 sp, ch 3, sc in next ch-3 sp, ch 3; repeat from ★ around; join with slip st to first sc: 18 sps.

Rnd 4: Slip st in next ch-9 sp, ch 3 **(counts as first dc)**, 6 dc in same sp, ch 7, slip st in top of last dc made *(Fig. 1a, page 58)*, 7 dc in same ch-9 sp, skip next 2 ch-3 sps, ★ 7 dc in next ch-9 sp, ch 7, slip st in top of last dc made, 7 dc in same ch-9 sp, skip next 2 ch-3 sps; repeat from ★ around; join with slip st to first dc: 84 dc and 6 ch-7 sps.

Rnd 5: Slip st in next 2 dc, ch 1, sc in same st, ★ † ch 3, skip next dc, sc in next dc, skip next 2 dc, 14 dc in next ch-7 sp, skip next 2 dc, sc in next dc, ch 3, skip next dc, sc in next dc †, ch 3, skip next 4 dc, sc in next dc; repeat from ★ 4 times **more**, then repeat from † to † once, ch 1, skip last 4 sts, hdc in first sc to form last ch-3 sp: 84 dc and 18 ch-3 sps.

Rnd 6: Ch 1, sc in last ch-3 sp made, ch 3, sc in next ch-3 sp, ch 3, ★ † skip next sc and next dc, sc in next dc, (ch 3, skip next dc, sc in next dc) twice, sc in next dc, ch 5, slip st in 5th ch from hook, ch 6, slip st in 6th ch from hook, ch 5, slip st in 5th ch from hook, sc in same dc as last sc made and in next dc, ch 3, (skip next dc, sc in next dc, ch 3) twice, skip next 2 dc and next sc †, (sc in next ch-3 sp, ch 3) 3 times; repeat from ★ 4 times **more**, then repeat from † to † once, sc in next ch-3 sp, ch 3; join with slip st to first sc, finish off.

See Starching, page 61. Use 6-Point Blocking Pattern, page 62.

17

EASY +

Finished Size: Approximately 5" (12.5 cm) diameter

INSTRUCTIONS

Rnd 1 (Right side)**:** Ch 3, 11 hdc in 3rd ch from hook; join with slip st to top of beginning ch-3: 12 sts.

Rnd 2: Ch 8, skip next hdc, ★ dc in next hdc, ch 5, skip next hdc; repeat from ★ around; join with slip st to 3rd ch of beginning ch-8: 6 ch-5 sps.

Rnd 3: (Slip st, ch 1, sc) in next ch-5 sp, ★ † ch 6, slip st in 4th ch from hook, 2 dc in same ch-5 sp, ch 4, slip st in 4th ch from hook, ch 5, slip st in 4th ch from hook, ch 6, slip st in 5th ch from hook, ch 7, slip st in 6th ch from hook, ch 8, slip st in 7th ch from hook, ch 7, slip st in 6th ch from hook, ch 6, slip st in 5th ch from hook, (ch 5, slip st in 4th ch from hook) twice, 2 dc in same ch-5 sp on Rnd 2 as previous dc, ch 4, slip st in 4th ch from hook, ch 2, sc in same ch-5 sp as last dc made †, sc in next ch-5 sp; repeat from ★ 4 times **more**, then repeat from † to † once; join with slip st to first sc, finish off.

See Starching, page 61. Use 6-Point Blocking Pattern, page 62.

18

EASY +

Finished Size: Approximately 3 1/4" (8.5 cm) diameter

INSTRUCTIONS

Rnd 1 (Right side)**:** Ch 4, 11 dc in 4th ch from hook; join with slip st to top of beginning ch-4: 12 sts.

Rnd 2: ★ † [Ch 14, slip st in 4th ch from hook, ch 10, slip st in st at base of ch-14 **(Picot loop made)]**, slip st in next dc, ch 15, slip st in 5th ch from hook to form a ring †, ch 10, slip st in dc at base of ch-15 and in next dc; repeat from ★ 4 times **more**, then repeat from † to † once, YO 8 times, insert hook in dc at base of ch-15, YO and pull up a loop (10 loops on hook), (YO and draw through 2 loops on hook) 9 times to form last ch-10 sp: 6 Picot loops and 6 rings.

Rnd 3: Slip st in last ch-10 sp made, ★ ch 15, skip next Picot loop, slip st in next ch-10 sp and in next ring, (ch 5, slip st in same ring) 5 times, slip st in next ch-10 sp; repeat from ★ around working last slip st in first slip st; finish off.

See Starching, page 61. Use 12-Point Blocking Pattern, page 63, pinning the Picots on Rnd 2 toward the center.

19

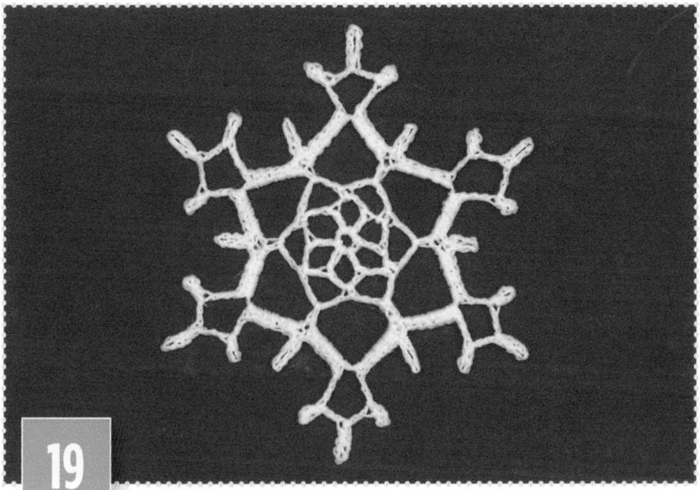

EASY +

Finished Size: Approximately $4^1/_4$" (11 cm) diameter

INSTRUCTIONS

Ch 6; join with slip st to form a ring.

Rnd 1 (Right side)**:** Ch 7, dc in ring, (ch 4, dc in ring) 4 times, ch 2, hdc in 3rd ch of beginning ch-7 to form last ch-4 sp: 6 ch-4 sps.

Rnd 2: Ch 1, sc in last ch-4 sp made, (ch 6, sc in next ch-4 sp) around, ch 3, dc in first sc to form last ch-6 sp.

Rnd 3: Ch 1, sc in last ch-6 made, ch 11, (sc in next ch-6 sp, ch 11) around; join with slip st to first sc: 6 loops.

Rnd 4: (Slip st, ch 1, 7 sc) in next loop, ★ † ch 7, slip st in 5th ch from hook, ch 9, slip st in 7th ch from hook, ch 7, slip st in 5th ch from hook, ch 2, 7 sc in same loop on Rnd 3 as previous sc, ch 6, slip st in top of last sc made ***(Fig. 1a, page 58)*** †, 7 sc in next loop; repeat from ★ 4 times **more**, then repeat from † to † once; join with slip st to first sc, finish off.

See Starching, page 61. Use 12-Point Blocking Pattern, page 63.

20

EASY +

Finished Size: Approximately $4^1/_2$" (11.5 cm) diameter

INSTRUCTIONS

Ch 5; join with slip st to form a ring.

Rnd 1 (Right side)**:** Ch 3 **(counts as first dc)**, dc in ring, ch 4, (3 dc in ring, ch 4) 5 times, dc in ring; join with slip st to first dc: 18 dc and 6 ch-4 sps.

Rnd 2: Ch 1, sc in same st as joining and in next dc, (sc, hdc, dc, hdc, sc) in next ch-4 sp, skip next dc, ★ sc in next 2 dc, (sc, hdc, dc, hdc, sc) in next ch-4 sp, skip next dc; repeat from ★ around; join with slip st to first sc: 42 sts.

Rnd 3: Ch 1, sc in same st as joining, ★ † ch 16, slip st in 8th ch from hook, ch 4, skip next 3 chs, slip st in next ch, ch 4, skip next 4 chs, sc in next sc, ch 5, skip next 2 sts, sc in next dc, ch 3, sc in next hdc, ch 5, skip next sc †, sc in next sc; repeat from ★ 4 times **more**, then repeat from † to † once; join with slip st to first sc, finish off.

See Starching, page 61. Use 12-Point Blocking Pattern, page 63.

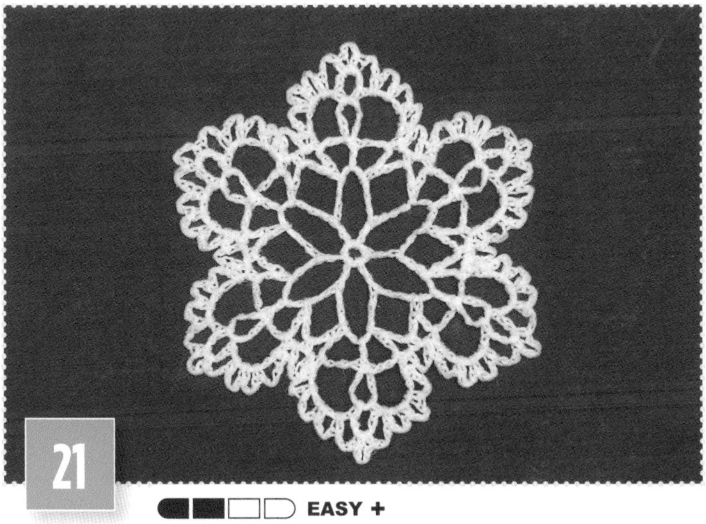

EASY +

Finished Size: Approximately 4" (10 cm) diameter

INSTRUCTIONS

Ch 5; join with slip st to form a ring.

Rnd 1 (Right side)**:** Ch 12, dc in ring, (ch 9, dc in ring) 4 times, ch 6, dc in 3rd ch of beginning ch-12 to form last ch-9 sp: 6 ch-9 sps.

Rnd 2: Ch 1, sc in last ch-9 sp made, ch 6, ★ (sc, ch 5, dc) in next ch-9 sp, ch 7, slip st in top of last dc made ***(Fig. 1a, page 58)***, ch 5, sc in same ch-9 sp, ch 6; repeat from ★ around, (sc, ch 5, dc) in same ch-9 sp as first sc, ch 7, slip st in top of last dc made, ch 2, dc in first sc to form last ch-5 sp: 24 sps.

Rnd 3: Ch 1, sc in last ch-5 sp made, (ch 1, sc in next sp) twice, ch 6, (sc, ch 5, sc) in next ch-7 sp, ch 6, ★ sc in next ch-5 sp, (ch 1, sc in next sp) twice, ch 6, (sc, ch 5, sc) in next ch-7 sp, ch 6; repeat from ★ around; join with slip st to first sc: 30 sps.

Rnd 4: (Slip st, ch 1, sc) in next ch-1 sp, ★ † ch 3, sc in next ch-1 sp, (sc, ch 3) 4 times in next ch-6 sp, (sc, ch 3, sc) in next ch-5 sp, (ch 3, sc) 4 times in next ch-6 sp †, sc in next ch-1 sp; repeat from ★ 4 times **more**, then repeat from † to † once; join with slip st to first sc, finish off.

See Starching, page 61. Use 6-Point Blocking Pattern, page 62.

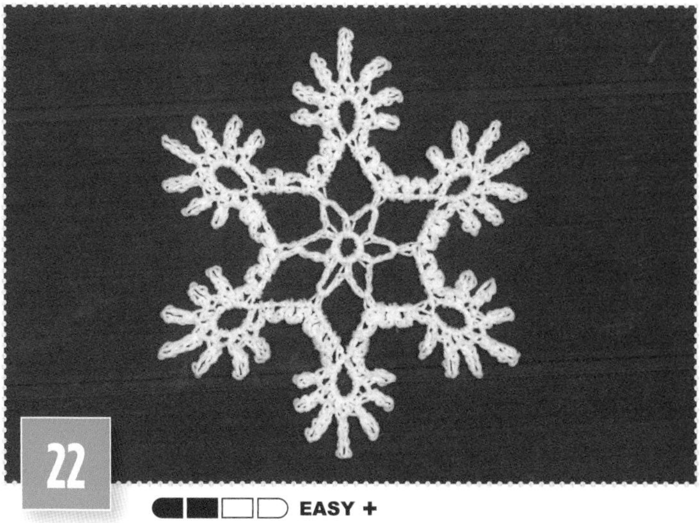

EASY +

Finished Size: Approximately 4" (10 cm) diameter

STITCH GUIDE

PICOT

Slip st in first ch made.

INSTRUCTIONS

Ch 6; join with slip st to form a ring.

Rnd 1 (Right side)**:** Ch 1, sc in ring, (ch 6, sc in ring) 5 times, ch 3, dc in first sc to form last ch-6 sp: 6 ch-6 sps.

Rnd 2: Ch 1, sc in last ch-6 sp made, ch 11, slip st in 7th ch from hook to form a ring, ch 4, ★ sc in next ch-6 sp, ch 11, slip st in 7th ch from hook, ch 4; repeat from ★ around; join with slip st to first sc: 6 rings and 12 ch-4 sps.

Rnd 3: (Slip st, ch 1, sc) in next ch-4 sp, ch 3, (sc, ch 3) twice in same sp, ★ † in next ring work [sc, ch 4, Picot, sc, ch 5, Picot, sc, ch 6, Picot, sc, ch 7, Picot, sc, ch 6, Picot, sc, ch 5, Picot, sc, ch 4, Picot, sc], (ch 3, sc) 3 times in next ch-4 sp †, (sc, ch 3) 3 times in next ch-4 sp; repeat from ★ 4 times **more**, then repeat from † to † once; join with slip st to first sc, finish off.

See Starching, page 61. Use 6-Point Blocking Pattern, page 62.

EASY +

Finished Size: Approximately $4^{1}/_{4}$" (11 cm) diameter

INSTRUCTIONS

Ch 6; join with slip st to form a ring.

Rnd 1 (Right side)**:** Ch 1, 12 sc in ring; join with slip st to first sc.

Rnd 2: Ch 1, sc in same st as joining, (ch 3, sc in next sc) around, ch 1, hdc in first sc to form last ch-3 sp: 12 ch-3 sps.

Rnds 3 and 4: Ch 1, sc in last ch-3 sp made, (ch 3, sc in next ch-3 sp) around, ch 1, hdc in first sc to form last ch-3 sp.

Rnd 5: Ch 1, sc in last ch-3 sp made, ch 16, skip next ch-3 sp, ★ sc in next ch-3 sp, ch 16, skip next ch-3 sp; repeat from ★ around; join with slip st to first sc: 6 loops.

Rnd 6: Slip st in next loop, ch 1, 17 sc in same loop and in each loop around; join with slip st to first sc: 102 sc.

Rnd 7: Slip st in next 3 sc, ch 1, sc in same st, ★ † ch 4, skip next 2 sc, sc in next sc, ch 4, skip next sc, sc in next sc, ch 5, slip st in 5th ch from hook, ch 6, slip st in 6th ch from hook, ch 5, slip st in 5th ch from hook, slip st in top of last sc made ***(Fig. 1a, page 58)***, ch 4, skip next sc, sc in next sc, ch 4, skip next 2 sc, sc in next sc, ch 5, skip next 6 sts †, sc in next sc; repeat from ★ 4 times **more**, then repeat from † to † once; join with slip st to first sc, finish off.

See Starching, page 61. Use 6-Point Blocking Pattern, page 62.

EASY +

Finished Size: Approximately $3^{1}/_{4}$" (8.5 cm) diameter

STITCH GUIDE

Treble Crochet *(tr)*
(Figs. 11a & b, page 60)

INSTRUCTIONS

Ch 8; join with slip st to form a ring.

Rnd 1 (Right side)**:** Ch 4, 23 tr in ring; join with slip st to top of beginning ch-4: 24 sts.

Rnd 2: Ch 3, dc in next tr, ★ † (ch 5, slip st in 4th ch from hook) 5 times, ch 1, skip next 2 tr †, dc in next 2 tr; repeat from ★ 4 times **more**, then repeat from † to † once; join with slip st to top of beginning ch-3, finish off.

See Starching, page 61. Use 6-Point Blocking Pattern, page 62.

25

EASY +

Finished Size: Approximately 2¾" (7 cm) diameter

STITCH GUIDE

Quadruple Triple Treble Crochet *(qtr)* ***(Figs. 14a & b, page 60)***

INSTRUCTIONS

Rnd 1 (Right side)**:** Ch 2, 12 sc in 2nd ch from hook; join with slip st to first sc.

Rnd 2: Ch 12, slip st in 4th ch from hook to form a ring, ★ ch 8, slip st in next 2 sc, ch 12, slip st in 4th ch from hook to form a ring; repeat from ★ around to last sc, ch 1, qtr in last sc to form last ch-8 sp: 12 ch-8 sps and 6 rings.

Rnd 3: Slip st in last ch-8 sp made, ★ ch 11, slip st in next ch-8 sp and in next ring, (ch 5, slip st in same ring) 5 times, slip st in next ch-8 sp; repeat from ★ around working last slip st in joining slip st, finish off.

See Starching, page 61. Use 6-Point Blocking Pattern, page 62.

26

EASY +

Finished Size: Approximately 4¼" (11 cm) diameter

STITCH GUIDE

Double Treble Crochet *(dtr)* ***(Figs. 12a & b, page 60)***

INSTRUCTIONS

Ch 6; join with slip st to form a ring.

Rnd 1 (Right side)**:** Ch 6, (dc in ring, ch 3) 11 times; join with slip st to 3rd ch of beginning ch-6: 12 ch-3 sps.

Rnd 2: Slip st in next ch-3 sp, ch 6, (dc in next ch-3 sp, ch 3) around; join with slip st to 3rd ch of beginning ch-6.

Rnd 3: Slip st in next ch-3 sp, ch 1, (sc in same sp, ch 5) twice, (sc, ch 5, sc) in next ch-3 sp, ★ (sc, ch 5) twice in next ch-3 sp, (sc, ch 5, sc) in next ch-3 sp; repeat from ★ around; join with slip st to first sc: 18 ch-5 sps.

Rnd 4: Ch 1, sc in same st as joining, ★ † ch 4, dc in next ch-5 sp, ch 3, (dtr, ch 7, dtr) in next ch-5 sp, ch 3, dc in next ch-5 sp, ch 4, skip next sc †, sc in next sc; repeat from ★ 4 times **more**, then repeat from † to † once; join with slip st to first sc, finish off.

See Starching, page 61. Use 6-Point Blocking Pattern, page 62.

27

EASY +

Finished Size: Approximately 4" (10 cm) diameter

STITCH GUIDE

Triple Treble Crochet *(tr tr)* ***(Figs. 13a & b, page 60)***

INSTRUCTIONS

Ch 6; join with slip st to form a ring.

Rnd 1 (Right side)**:** Ch 7, (dc in ring, ch 4) 11 times; join with slip st to 3rd ch of beginning ch-7: 12 ch-4 sps.

Rnd 2: (Slip st, ch 1, sc) in next ch-4 sp, ch 3, sc in same sp, ch 5, ★ (sc, ch 3, sc) in each of next 2 ch-4 sps, ch 5; repeat from ★ around to last ch-4 sp, (sc, ch 3, sc) in last ch-4 sp; join with slip st to first sc: 18 sps.

Rnd 3: Ch 1, sc in same st as joining, ★ † ch 6, dc in next ch-3 sp, ch 4, (tr tr, ch 9, tr tr) in next ch-5 sp, ch 4, dc in next ch-3 sp, ch 6, skip next sc †, sc in next sc; repeat from ★ 4 times **more**, then repeat from † to † once; join with slip st to first sc, finish off.

See Starching, page 61. Use 6-Point Blocking Pattern, page 62.

28

EASY +

Finished Size: Approximately 3$^{1}/_{4}$" (8.5 cm) diameter

STITCH GUIDE

Treble Crochet *(tr)* ***(Figs. 11a & b, page 60)***

INSTRUCTIONS

Ch 5; join with slip st to form a ring.

Rnd 1 (Right side)**:** Ch 1, sc in ring, (ch 7, sc in ring) 5 times, ch 3, tr in first sc to form last ch-7 sp: 6 ch-7 sps.

Rnd 2: Ch 1, sc in last ch-7 sp made, ch 9, (sc in next ch-7 sp, ch 9) around; join with slip st to first sc.

Rnd 3: (Slip st, 4 sc, ch 3, 4 sc, slip st) in each ch-9 sp around; join with slip st to first slip st: 60 sts and 6 ch-3 sps.

Rnd 4: Ch 15, skip next ch-3 sp and next 5 sts, ★ slip st in next slip st, ch 15, skip next ch-3 sp and next 5 sts; repeat from ★ around; join with slip st to joining slip st: 6 loops.

Rnd 5: In each loop work (slip st, 2 sc, ch 3, 2 sc, ch 4, 2 sc, ch 5, 2 sc, ch 6, 2 sc, ch 5, 2 sc, ch 4, 2 sc, ch 3, 2 sc, slip st); join with slip st to first slip st, finish off.

See Starching, page 61. Use 6-Point Blocking Pattern, page 62.

29

EASY +

Finished Size: Approximately 3$^{1}/_{2}$" (9 cm) diameter

STITCH GUIDE

Treble Crochet *(tr)* ***(Figs. 11a & b, page 60)***

INSTRUCTIONS

Rnd 1 (Right side)**:** Ch 3, 11 hdc in 3rd ch from hook; join with slip st to top of beginning ch-3: 12 sts.

Rnd 2: Ch 9, slip st in 4th ch from hook **(Picot made)**, ★ ch 5, skip next hdc, slip st in next hdc, ch 9, slip st in 4th ch from hook; repeat from ★ around to last hdc, ch 1, skip last hdc, tr in joining slip st to form last ch-5 sp: 12 ch-5 sps and 6 Picots.

Rnd 3: Ch 1, sc in last tr made, ★ † ch 7, slip st in 4th ch from hook, ch 3, sc in 4th ch of next ch-5 sp, (ch 5, slip st in 4th ch from hook) twice, ch 6, slip st in 5th ch from hook, (ch 5, slip st in 4th ch from hook) twice, ch 1, skip next Picot and next ch †, sc in next ch; repeat from ★ 4 times **more**, then repeat from † to † once; join with slip st to first sc, finish off.

See Starching, page 61. Use 12-Point Blocking Pattern, page 63.

30

EASY +

Finished Size: Approximately 3$^{1}/_{2}$" (9 cm) diameter

STITCH GUIDE

Treble Crochet *(tr)* ***(Figs. 11a & b, page 60)***

INSTRUCTIONS

Rnd 1 (Right side)**:** Ch 3, 11 hdc in 3rd ch from hook; join with slip st to top of beginning ch-3: 12 sts.

Rnd 2: Ch 8, skip next hdc, ★ dc in next hdc, ch 5, skip next hdc; repeat from ★ around; join with slip st to 3rd ch of beginning ch-8: 6 ch-5 sps.

Rnd 3: (Slip st, ch 1, sc) in next ch-5 sp, ★ † (ch 3, sc in same sp) twice, ch 4, tr in same sp, ch 4, tr in top of last tr made ***(Fig. 1a, page 58)***, ch 6, slip st in 6th ch from hook, ch 4, tr in 4th ch from hook, (tr, ch 4, sc) in same ch-5 sp, (ch 3, sc in same sp) twice †, sc in next ch-5 sp; repeat from ★ 4 times **more**, then repeat from † to † once; join with slip st to first sc, finish off.

See Starching, page 61. Use 6-Point Blocking Pattern, page 62.

31

EASY +

Finished Size: Approximately 3" (7.5 cm) diameter

STITCH GUIDE

Quadruple Treble Crochet *(qtr)* ***(Figs. 14a & b, page 60)***

INSTRUCTIONS

Ch 5; join with slip st to form a ring.

Rnd 1 (Right side)**:** ★ Ch 8, qtr in ring, (ch 5, slip st in 5th ch from hook) twice, ch 6, slip st in 6th ch from hook, (ch 5, slip st in 5th ch from hook) twice, slip st in top of last qtr made ***(Fig. 1a, page 58)***, ch 8, slip st in ring; repeat from ★ 5 times **more**; finish off.

See Starching, page 61. Use 12-Point Blocking Pattern, page 63.

32

EASY +

Finished Size: Approximately 4 1/2" (11.5 cm) diameter

STITCH GUIDE

Treble Crochet *(tr)* ***(Figs. 11a & b, page 60)***

Triple Treble Crochet *(tr tr)* ***(Figs. 13a & b, page 60)***

INSTRUCTIONS

Ch 6; join with slip st to form a ring.

Rnd 1 (Right side)**:** Ch 5, (dc in ring, ch 2) 11 times; join with slip st to 3rd ch of beginning ch-5: 12 ch-2 sps.

Rnd 2: (Slip st, ch 3, slip st) in each ch-2 sp around; join with slip st to first slip st.

Rnd 3: Ch 5, skip next ch-3 sp and next slip st, ★ slip st in next slip st, ch 5, skip next ch-3 sp and next slip st; repeat from ★ around; join with slip st to joining slip st.

Rnd 4: Ch 7, skip next ch-5 sp, ★ hdc in next slip st, ch 5, skip next ch-5 sp; repeat from ★ around; join with slip st to 2nd ch of beginning ch-7.

Rnd 5: (Slip st, ch 1, sc) in next ch-5 sp, (ch 5, sc in same sp) twice, ★ sc in next ch-5 sp, (ch 5, sc in same sp) twice; repeat from ★ around; join with slip st to first sc: 24 ch-5 sps.

Rnd 6: Ch 1, sc in same st as joining, ★ † ch 5, tr in next ch-5 sp, ch 5, tr tr in next ch-5 sp, ch 7, tr tr in next ch-5 sp, ch 5, tr in next ch-5 sp, ch 5, skip next sc †, sc in next sc; repeat from ★ 4 times **more**, then repeat from † to † once; join with slip st to first sc, finish off.

See Starching, page 61. Use 6-Point Blocking Pattern, page 62.

EASY +

EASY +

Finished Size: Approximately 5" (12.5 cm) diameter

STITCH GUIDE

Treble Crochet *(tr)* *(Figs. 11a & b, page 60)*

Triple Treble Crochet *(tr tr)* *(Figs. 13a & b, page 60)*

The first 3 rounds of this snowflake are the same as #32. The last 3 rounds have been changed for a completely different look.

INSTRUCTIONS

Ch 6; join with slip st to form a ring.

Rnd 1 (Right side)**:** Ch 5, (dc in ring, ch 2) 11 times; join with slip st to 3rd ch of beginning ch-5: 12 ch-2 sps.

Rnd 2: (Slip st, ch 3, slip st) in each ch-2 sp around; join with slip st to first slip st.

Rnd 3: Ch 5, skip next ch-3 sp and next slip st, ★ slip st in next slip st, ch 5, skip next ch-3 sp and next slip st; repeat from ★ around; join with slip st to joining slip st.

Rnd 4: Ch 8, skip next ch-5 sp, ★ dc in next slip st, ch 5, skip next ch-5 sp; repeat from ★ around; join with slip st to 3rd ch of beginning ch-8.

Rnd 5: (Slip st, ch 1, sc) in next ch-5 sp, (ch 5, sc in same sp) twice, ★ sc in next ch-5 sp, (ch 5, sc in same sp) twice; repeat from ★ around; join with slip st to first sc: 24 ch-5 sps.

Rnd 6: Ch 1, sc in same st as joining, ★ † ch 6, tr in next ch-5 sp, ch 5, tr tr in next ch-5 sp, [ch 4, slip st in 4th ch from hook, ch 6, slip st in 6th ch from hook, ch 4, slip st in 4th ch from hook **(3-Picot group made)]**, slip st in ch at base of first Picot, tr tr in next ch-5 sp, ch 5, tr in next ch-5 sp, ch 6, skip next sc †, sc in next sc; repeat from ★ 4 times **more**, then repeat from † to † once; join with slip st to first sc, finish off.

See Starching, page 61. Use 6-Point Blocking Pattern, page 62.

Finished Size: Approximately 3½" (9 cm) diameter

INSTRUCTIONS

Ch 5; join with slip st to form a ring.

Rnd 1 (Right side)**:** Ch 6, dc in ring, (ch 3, dc in ring) 10 times, ch 1, hdc in 3rd ch of beginning ch-6 to form last ch-3 sp: 12 ch-3 sps.

Rnd 2: Ch 1, sc in last ch-3 sp made, ch 14, sc in next ch-3 sp, ★ ch 3, sc in next ch-3 sp, ch 14, sc in next ch-3 sp; repeat from ★ around, ch 1, hdc in first sc to form last ch-3 sp: 6 ch-3 sps and 6 loops.

Rnd 3: Ch 1, sc in last ch-3 sp made and in next loop, ★ † (ch 3, sc in same loop) 5 times, ch 6, slip st in top of last sc made *(Fig. 1a, page 58)*, sc in same loop, (ch 3, sc in same loop) 5 times †, sc in next ch-3 sp and in next loop; repeat from ★ 4 times **more**, then repeat from † to † once; join with slip st to first sc, finish off.

See Starching, page 61. Use 6-Point Blocking Pattern, page 62.

EASY +

Finished Size: Approximately 4¾" (12 cm) diameter

STITCH GUIDE

Treble Crochet *(tr)*
(Figs. 11a & b, page 60)

Triple Treble Crochet *(tr tr)*
(Figs. 13a & b, page 60)

The first 5 rounds of this snowflake are the same as #33, page 21. The last round has been changed for a slightly different look.

INSTRUCTIONS

Ch 6; join with slip st to form a ring.

Rnd 1 (Right side)**:** Ch 5, (dc in ring, ch 2) 11 times; join with slip st to 3rd ch of beginning ch-5: 12 ch-2 sps.

Rnd 2: (Slip st, ch 3, slip st) in each ch-2 sp around; join with slip st to first slip st.

Rnd 3: Ch 5, skip next ch-3 sp and next slip st, ★ slip st in next slip st, ch 5, skip next ch-3 sp and next slip st; repeat from ★ around; join with slip st to joining slip st.

Rnd 4: Ch 8, skip next ch-5 sp, ★ dc in next slip st, ch 5, skip next ch-5 sp; repeat from ★ around; join with slip st to 3rd ch of beginning ch-8.

Rnd 5: (Slip st, ch 1, sc) in next ch-5 sp, (ch 5, sc in same sp) twice, ★ sc in next ch-5 sp, (ch 5, sc in same sp) twice; repeat from ★ around; join with slip st to first sc: 24 ch-5 sps.

Rnd 6: Ch 1, sc in same st as joining, ★ † ch 5, tr in next ch-5 sp, ch 5, tr tr in next ch-5 sp, ch 7, slip st in 7th ch from hook, tr tr in next ch-5 sp, ch 5, tr in next ch-5 sp, ch 5, skip next sc †, sc in next sc; repeat from ★ 4 times **more**, then repeat from † to † once; join with slip st to first sc, finish off.

See Starching, page 61. Use 6-Point Blocking Pattern, page 62.

EASY +

Finished Size: Approximately 4" (10 cm) diameter

STITCH GUIDE

Double Treble Crochet *(dtr)*
(Figs. 12a & b, page 60)

INSTRUCTIONS

Ch 5; join with slip st to form a ring.

Rnd 1 (Right side)**:** Ch 5, (dc in ring, ch 2) 11 times; join with slip st to 3rd ch of beginning ch-5: 12 ch-2 sps.

Rnd 2: Slip st in next ch-2 sp, ch 10 **(counts as first dtr plus ch 5)**, slip st in 5th ch from hook, ★ † dtr in same ch-2 sp, ch 17, slip st in 11th ch from hook, (ch 11, slip st in 11th ch from hook) twice, ch 6, skip next ch-2 sp †, dtr in next ch-2 sp, ch 5, slip st in 5th ch from hook; repeat from ★ 4 times **more**, then repeat from † to † once; join with slip st to first dtr, finish off.

See Starching, page 61. Use 12-Point Blocking Pattern, page 63.

37 EASY +

Finished Size: Approximately 4½" (11.5 cm) diameter

INSTRUCTIONS

Ch 6; join with slip st to form a ring.

Rnd 1 (Right side)**:** Ch 1, sc in ring, (ch 5, sc in ring) 5 times, ch 2, dc in first sc to form last ch-5 sp: 6 ch-5 sps.

Rnd 2: Ch 1, sc in last ch-5 sp made, ch 13, slip st in 9th ch from hook to form a ring, ch 4, ★ sc in next ch-5 sp, ch 13, slip st in 9th ch from hook, ch 4; repeat from ★ around; join with slip st to first sc: 6 rings and 12 ch-4 sps.

Rnd 3: (Slip st, ch 1, sc) in next ch-4 sp, ★ † (ch 3, sc in same sp) 3 times, ch 5, (sc, ch 5, 2 dc) in next ring, ch 6, slip st in 5th ch from hook, ch 1, (2 dc, ch 5, sc) in same ring, ch 5, sc in next ch-4 sp, (ch 3, sc in same sp) 3 times †, sc in next ch-4 sp; repeat from ★ 4 times **more**, then repeat from † to † once; join with slip st to first sc, finish off.

See Starching, page 61. Use 6-Point Blocking Pattern, page 62.

38 EASY +

Finished Size: Approximately 6" (15 cm) diameter

STITCH GUIDE

Treble Crochet *(tr)*
(Figs. 11a & b, page 60)

Double Treble Crochet *(dtr)*
(Figs. 12a & b, page 60)

INSTRUCTIONS

Ch 5; join with slip st to form a ring.

Rnd 1 (Right side)**:** Ch 12, dc in ring, (ch 9, dc in ring) 4 times, ch 4, dtr in 3rd ch of beginning ch-12 to form last ch-9 sp: 6 ch-9 sps.

Rnd 2: Ch 3 **(counts as first dc, now and throughout)**, (2 dc, ch 3, 3 dc) in top of last dtr made, ch 9, ★ (3 dc, ch 3, 3 dc) in center ch of next ch-9, ch 9; repeat from ★ around; join with slip st to first dc: 36 dc, 6 ch-3 sps, and 6 ch-9 sps.

Rnd 3: Slip st in next 2 dc and in next ch-3 sp, ch 3, (2 dc, ch 3, 3 dc) in same sp, ch 6, (tr, ch 5, tr) in center ch of next ch-9, ch 6, ★ (3 dc, ch 3, 3 dc) in next ch-3 sp, ch 6, (tr, ch 5, tr) in center ch of next ch-9, ch 6; repeat from ★ around; join with slip st to first dc.

Rnd 4: Slip st in next 2 dc and in next ch-3 sp, ch 2, (hdc, dc, hdc, ch 2, slip st) in same sp, ★ † ch 9, skip next ch-6 sp, tr in center ch of next ch-5, ch 4, slip st in 4th ch from hook, ch 6, slip st in 6th ch from hook, ch 4, slip st in 4th ch from hook, tr in same ch as last tr made, ch 9, skip next ch-6 sp †, (slip st, ch 2, hdc, dc, hdc, ch 2, slip st) in next ch-3 sp; repeat from ★ 4 times **more**, then repeat from † to † once; join with slip st in slip st at base of beginning ch-2, finish off.

See Starching, page 61. Use 12-Point Blocking Pattern, page 63.

39

EASY +

Finished Size: Approximately 4¹/₄" (11 cm) diameter

STITCH GUIDE

Treble Crochet *(tr)* ***(Figs. 11a & b, page 60)***

INSTRUCTIONS

Ch 5; join with slip st to form a ring.

Rnd 1 (Right side)**:** Ch 1, sc in ring, (ch 6, sc in ring) 5 times, ch 3, dc in first sc to form last ch-6 sp: 6 ch-6 sps.

Rnd 2: Ch 1, sc in last ch-6 sp made, ch 11, slip st in 7th ch from hook to form a ring, ch 4, ★ sc in next ch-6 sp, ch 11, slip st in 7th ch from hook, ch 4; repeat from ★ around; join with slip st to first sc: 6 sc, 6 rings, and 12 ch-4 sps.

Rnd 3: Ch 1, sc in same st as joining, ★ † ch 6, skip next ch-4 sp, tr in next ring, (ch 6, slip st in 5th ch from hook, ch 1, tr in same ring) 6 times, ch 6, skip next ch-4 sp †, sc in next sc; repeat from ★ 4 times **more**, then repeat from † to † once; join with slip st to first sc, finish off.

See Starching, page 61. Use 6-Point Blocking Pattern, page 62.

40

EASY +

Finished Size: Approximately 5" (12.5 cm) diameter

STITCH GUIDE

Treble Crochet *(tr)* ***(Figs. 11a & b, page 60)***
Double Treble Crochet *(dtr)* ***(Figs. 12a & b, page 60)***

INSTRUCTIONS

Ch 6; join with slip st to form a ring.

Rnd 1 (Right side)**:** Ch 3 **(counts as first dc, now and throughout)**, 23 dc in ring; join with slip st to first dc: 24 dc.

Rnd 2: Ch 3, (dc, ch 2, 2 dc) in same st as joining, ch 3, skip next dc, sc in next dc, ch 3, skip next dc, ★ (2 dc, ch 2, 2 dc) in next dc, ch 3, skip next dc, sc in next dc, ch 3, skip next dc; repeat from ★ around; join with slip st to first dc: 24 dc and 18 sps.

Rnd 3: Slip st in next dc and in next ch-2 sp, ★ † ch 3, 2 dc in same sp, ch 6, (tr, dtr) in 4th ch from hook, ch 9, slip st in 6th ch from hook, ch 3, (dtr, tr, ch 3, slip st) in same ch as last dtr made, slip st in next 2 chs and in top of last dc made ***(Fig. 1a, page 58)***, (2 dc, ch 3, slip st) in same ch-2 sp on Rnd 2 as previous dc, slip st in next 2 dc and in next ch-3 sp, ch 7, slip st in 6th ch from hook, ch 1, slip st in next ch-3 sp †, slip st in next 2 dc and in next ch-2 sp; repeat from ★ 4 times **more**, then repeat from † to † once; join with slip st to joining slip st, finish off.

See Starching, page 61. Use 12-Point Blocking Pattern, page 63.

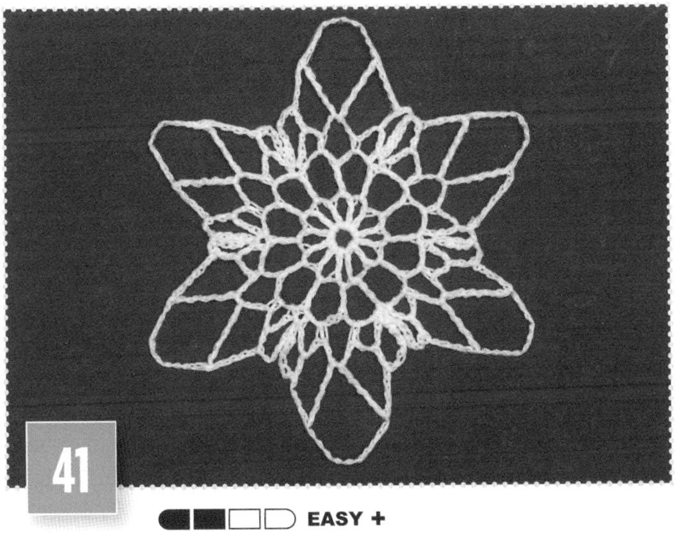

EASY +

Finished Size: Approximately $4\frac{1}{2}$" (11.5 cm) diameter

STITCH GUIDE

Triple Treble Crochet *(tr tr)* ***(Figs. 13a & b, page 60)***

INSTRUCTIONS

Ch 6; join with slip st to form a ring.

Rnd 1 (Right side)**:** Ch 5, (dc in ring, ch 2) 11 times; join with slip st to 3rd ch of beginning ch-5: 12 ch-2 sps.

Rnd 2: Slip st in next ch-2 sp, ch 7, (dc in next ch-2 sp, ch 4) around; join with slip st to 3rd ch of beginning ch-7.

Rnd 3: Slip st in next ch-4 sp, ch 1, (sc in same sp, ch 5) twice, (sc, ch 5, sc) in next ch-4 sp, ★ (sc, ch 5) twice in next ch-4 sp, (sc, ch 5, sc) in next ch-4 sp; repeat from ★ around; join with slip st to first sc: 18 ch-5 sps.

Rnd 4: Ch 1, sc in same st as joining, ★ † ch 5, dc in next ch-5 sp, ch 4, (tr tr, ch 9, tr tr) in next ch-5 sp, ch 4, dc in next ch-5 sp, ch 5, skip next sc †, sc in next sc; repeat from ★ 4 times **more**, then repeat from † to † once; join with slip st to first sc, finish off.

See Starching, page 61. Use 6-Point Blocking Pattern, page 62.

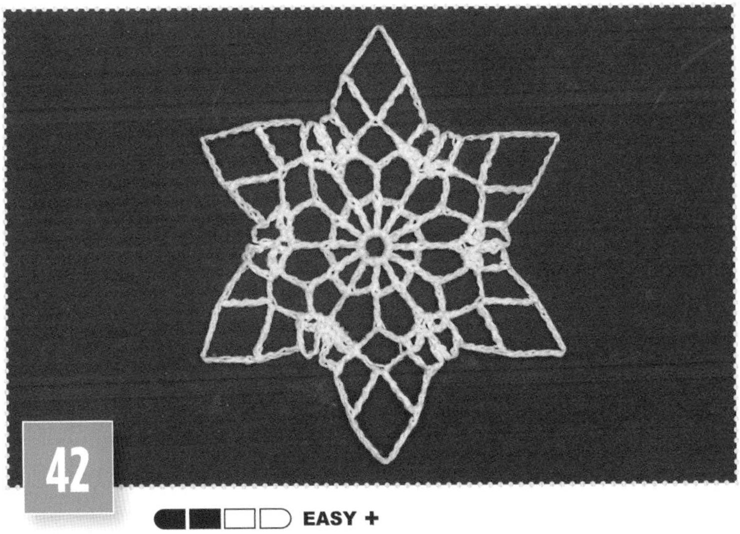

EASY +

Finished Size: Approximately $4\frac{1}{4}$" (11 cm) diameter

STITCH GUIDE

Double Treble Crochet *(dtr)* ***(Figs. 12a & b, page 60)***

INSTRUCTIONS

Ch 6; join with slip st to form a ring.

Rnd 1 (Right side)**:** Ch 6 **(counts as first dc plus ch 3)**, (dc in ring, ch 3) 11 times; join with slip st to first dc: 12 dc.

Rnd 2: Ch 8, (dc in next dc, ch 5) around; join with slip st to 3rd ch of beginning ch-8: 12 ch-5 sps.

Rnd 3: Slip st in next ch-5 sp, ch 1, (sc, ch 3, sc) in same sp, ch 5, ★ (sc, ch 3, sc) in each of next 2 ch-5 sps, ch 5; repeat from ★ around to last ch-5 sp, (sc, ch 3, sc) in last sp; join with slip st to first sc: 18 sps.

Rnd 4: Ch 1, sc in same st as joining, ★ † ch 4, skip next ch-3 sp, dc in next ch-5 sp, ch 3, (dtr, ch 9, dtr) in center ch of same ch-5, ch 3, dc in same ch-5 sp, ch 4, skip next ch-3 sp and next sc †, sc in next sc; repeat from ★ 4 times **more**, then repeat from † to † once; join with slip st to first sc, finish off.

See Starching, page 61. Use 6-Point Blocking Pattern, page 62.

43

EASY +

Finished Size: Approximately 5¼" (13.5 cm) diameter

STITCH GUIDE

Treble Crochet *(tr)* ***(Figs. 11a & b, page 60)***

Double Treble Crochet *(dtr)* ***(Figs. 12a & b, page 60)***

INSTRUCTIONS

Ch 6; join with slip st to form a ring.

Rnd 1 (Right side)**:** Ch 10, dtr in ring, (ch 5, dtr in ring) 10 times, ch 2, dc in 5th ch of beginning ch-10 to form last ch-5 sp: 12 ch-5 sps.

Rnd 2: Ch 1, sc in last ch-5 sp made, (ch 5, sc in next ch-5 sp) around, ch 2, dc in first sc to form last ch-5 sp.

Rnd 3: Ch 1, sc in last ch-5 sp made, (ch 7, sc in next ch-5 sp) around, ch 3, tr in first sc to form last ch-7 sp.

Rnd 4: Ch 1, sc in last ch-7 sp made, ★ † (ch 4, slip st in 3rd ch from hook) 3 times, ch 1, tr in center ch of next ch-7, (ch 4, slip st in 3rd ch from hook) 7 times, ch 1, tr in same center ch on Rnd 3 as previous tr, (ch 4, slip st in 3rd ch from hook) 3 times, ch 1 †, sc in center ch of next ch-7; repeat from ★ 4 times **more**, then repeat from † to † once; join with slip st to first sc, finish off.

See Starching, page 61. Use 6-Point Blocking Pattern, page 62.

44

EASY +

Finished Size: Approximately 4" (10 cm) diameter

STITCH GUIDE

Treble Crochet *(tr)* ***(Figs. 11a & b, page 60)***

INSTRUCTIONS

Ch 8; join with slip st to form a ring.

Rnd 1 (Right side)**:** Ch 4 **(counts as first tr, now and throughout)**, 23 tr in ring; join with slip st to first tr: 24 tr.

Rnd 2: Ch 1, sc in same st as joining and in next tr, ch 3, sc in next tr, ch 3, ★ sc in next 3 tr, ch 3, sc in next tr, ch 3; repeat from ★ around to last tr, sc in last tr; join with slip st to first sc: 24 sc and 12 ch-3 sps.

Rnd 3: Ch 3 **(counts as first dc)**, dc in same st as joining, ★ † (ch 4, slip st in 3rd ch from hook) 5 times, ch 1, skip next 2 ch-3 sps and next sc †, 2 dc in next sc; repeat from ★ 4 times **more**, then repeat from † to † once; join with slip st to first dc: 12 dc and 6 loops.

Rnd 4: (Slip st, ch 4, tr) in next dc, (ch 4, slip st in 3rd ch from hook) 7 times, ch 1, ★ skip next loop and next dc, 2 tr in next dc, (ch 4, slip st in 3rd ch from hook) 7 times, ch 1; repeat from ★ 4 times **more**, skip last loop and last st; join with slip st to first tr, finish off.

See Starching, page 61. Use 6-Point Blocking Pattern, page 62.

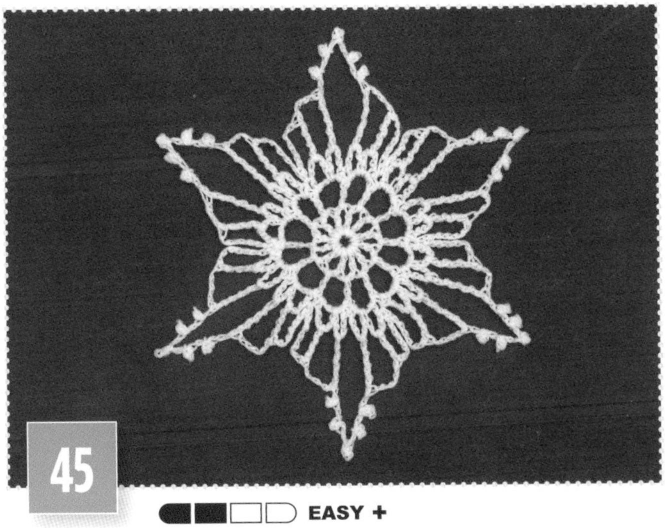

EASY +

Finished Size: Approximately 4 1/2" (11.5 cm) diameter

STITCH GUIDE

Treble Crochet *(tr)* ***(Figs. 11a & b, page 60)***

Triple Treble Crochet *(tr tr)* ***(Figs. 13a & b, page 60)***

INSTRUCTIONS

Ch 6; join with slip st to form a ring.

Rnd 1 (Right side)**:** Ch 5 **(counts as first dc plus ch 2)**, (dc in ring, ch 2) 11 times; join with slip st to first dc: 12 dc.

Rnd 2: Ch 7, (dc in next dc, ch 4) around; join with slip st to 3rd ch of beginning ch-7: 12 ch-4 sps.

Rnd 3: (Slip st, ch 1, sc) in next ch-4 sp, (ch 5, sc in same sp) twice, ★ sc in next ch-4 sp, (ch 5, sc in same sp) twice; repeat from ★ around; join with slip st to first sc: 24 ch-5 sps.

Rnd 4: Ch 1, sc in same st as joining, ★ † ch 6, tr in next ch-5 sp, ch 3, tr tr in next ch-5 sp, (ch 4, slip st in 3rd ch from hook) 5 times, ch 1, tr tr in next ch-5 sp, ch 3, tr in next ch-5 sp, ch 6, skip next sc †, sc in next sc; repeat from ★ 4 times **more**, then repeat from † to † once; join with slip st to first sc, finish off.

See Starching, page 61. Use 6-Point Blocking Pattern, page 62.

EASY +

Finished Size: Approximately 4 1/2" (11.5 cm) diameter

STITCH GUIDE

Treble Crochet *(tr)* ***(Figs. 11a & b, page 60)***

INSTRUCTIONS

Ch 8; join with slip st to form a ring.

Rnd 1 (Right side)**:** Ch 4 **(counts as first tr, now and throughout)**, 23 tr in ring; join with slip st to first tr: 24 tr.

Rnd 2: Ch 1, sc in same st as joining and in next tr, ch 3, sc in next tr, ch 3, ★ sc in next 3 tr, ch 3, sc in next tr, ch 3; repeat from ★ around to last tr, sc in last tr; join with slip st to first sc: 24 sc and 12 ch-3 sps.

Rnd 3: Ch 3 **(counts as first dc)**, dc in same st as joining, ★ † (ch 4, slip st in 3rd ch from hook) twice, ch 6, slip st in 3rd ch from hook, ch 4, slip st in 3rd ch from hook, ch 1, skip next 2 ch-3 sps and next sc †, 2 dc in next sc; repeat from ★ 4 times **more**, then repeat from † to † once; join with slip st to first dc: 12 dc and 6 loops.

Rnd 4: (Slip st, ch 4, tr) in next dc, ★ † (ch 4, slip st in 3rd ch from hook) 3 times, ch 1, (tr, ch 6, slip st in 6th ch from hook, tr) in center ch of next loop, (ch 4, slip st in 3rd ch from hook) 3 times, ch 1, skip next dc †, 2 tr in next dc; repeat from ★ 4 times **more**, then repeat from † to † once; join with slip st to first tr, finish off.

See Starching, page 61. Use 6-Point Blocking Pattern, page 62.

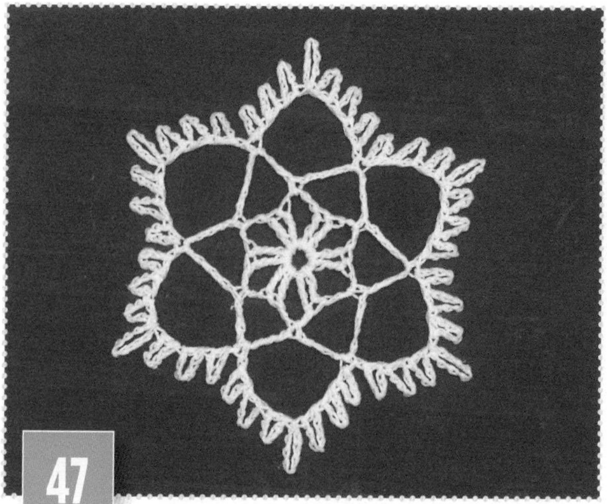

47

EASY +

Finished Size: Approximately 4" (10 cm) diameter

STITCH GUIDE

Treble Crochet *(tr)* ***(Figs. 11a & b, page 60)***
Double Treble Crochet *(dtr)* ***(Figs. 12a & b, page 60)***

INSTRUCTIONS

Ch 6; join with slip st to form a ring.

Rnd 1 (Right side)**:** Ch 4, tr in ring, (ch 3, 2 tr in ring) 5 times, ch 1, hdc in top of beginning ch-4 to form last ch-3 sp: 6 ch-3 sps.

Rnd 2: Ch 1, sc in last ch-3 sp made, (ch 9, sc in next ch-3 sp) around, ch 4, dtr in first sc to form last ch-9 sp: 6 ch-9 sps.

Rnd 3: Ch 1, sc in last ch-9 sp made, ★ † (ch 6, hdc in 6th ch from hook) 3 times, ch 8, slip st in 8th ch from hook, (ch 6, hdc in 6th ch from hook) 3 times †, sc in next ch-9 sp; repeat from ★ 4 times **more**, then repeat from † to † once; join with slip st to first sc, finish off.

See Starching, page 61. Use 6-Point Blocking Pattern, page 62.

48

EASY +

Finished Size: Approximately 4½" (11.5 cm) diameter

STITCH GUIDE

Treble Crochet *(tr)* ***(Figs. 11a & b, page 60)***

INSTRUCTIONS

Ch 5; join with slip st to form a ring.

Rnd 1 (Right side)**:** Ch 2 **(counts as first hdc)**, 11 hdc in ring; join with slip st to first hdc: 12 hdc.

Rnd 2: Ch 1, sc in same st as joining, ch 4, skip next hdc, ★ sc in next hdc, ch 4, skip next hdc; repeat from ★ around; join with slip st to first sc: 6 sc and 6 ch-4 sps.

Rnd 3: Ch 4, dc in next ch-4 sp, ★ (tr, ch 17, tr) in next sc, dc in next ch-4 sp; repeat from ★ around, tr in same st as beginning ch-4, ch 17; join with slip st to top of beginning ch-4: 18 sts and 6 loops.

Rnd 4: Slip st in next dc, ★ † ch 10, slip st in 7th ch from hook and in next 3 chs, slip st in next tr, 11 sc in next loop, ch 6, slip st in top of last sc made ***(Fig. 1a, page 58)***, 3 sc in same loop, [ch 7, slip st in 5th ch from hook, (ch 5, slip st in 5th ch from hook) twice **(3-Picot group made)**], slip st in ch at base of first Picot and in next 2 chs, 3 sc in same loop, ch 6, slip st in top of last sc made, 11 sc in same loop †, slip st in next tr and in next dc; repeat from ★ 4 times **more**, then repeat from † to † once; join with slip st to joining slip st, finish off.

See Starching, page 61. Use 12-Point Blocking Pattern, page 63.

49

EASY +

Finished Size: Approximately 3" (7.5 cm) diameter

STITCH GUIDE

Treble Crochet *(tr)* ***(Figs. 11a & b, page 60)***

INSTRUCTIONS

Ch 8; join with slip st to form a ring.

Rnd 1 (Right side)**:** Ch 4 **(counts as first tr)**, 23 tr in ring; join with slip st to first tr: 24 tr.

Rnd 2: Ch 1, sc in same st as joining, slip st in next tr, (ch 4, slip st in next tr) twice, ★ sc in next tr, slip st in next tr, (ch 4, slip st in next tr) twice; repeat from ★ around; join with slip st to first sc: 6 sc and 12 ch-4 sps.

Rnd 3: Ch 3, dc in same st as joining, ★ † (ch 4, slip st in 3rd ch from hook) 5 times, ch 1, skip next 2 ch-4 sps and next slip st †, 2 dc in next sc; repeat from ★ 4 times **more**, then repeat from † to † once; join with slip st to top of beginning ch-3, finish off.

See Starching, page 61. Use 6-Point Blocking Pattern, page 62.

50

EASY +

Finished Size: Approximately 4 1/4" (11 cm) diameter

STITCH GUIDE

Double Treble Crochet *(dtr)* ***(Figs. 12a & b, page 60)***

INSTRUCTIONS

Ch 6; join with slip st to form a ring.

Rnd 1 (Right side)**:** Ch 5, (dc in ring, ch 2) 11 times; join with slip st to 3rd ch of beginning ch-5: 12 ch-2 sps.

Rnd 2: Slip st in next ch-2 sp, ch 8, (dc in next ch-2 sp, ch 5) around; join with slip st to 3rd ch of beginning ch-8.

Rnd 3: (Slip st, ch 1, sc) in next ch-5 sp, (ch 5, sc in same sp) twice, ★ sc in next ch-5 sp, (ch 5, sc in same sp) twice; repeat from ★ around; join with slip st to first sc: 24 ch-5 sps.

Rnd 4: Ch 1, sc in same st as joining, ★ † ch 4, dc in next ch-5 sp, ch 4, dtr in next ch-5 sp, ch 9, dtr in next ch-5 sp, ch 4, dc in next ch-5 sp, ch 4, skip next sc †, sc in next sc; repeat from ★ 4 times **more**, then repeat from † to † once; join with slip st to first sc, finish off.

See Starching, page 61. Use 6-Point Blocking Pattern, page 62.

51

EASY +

Finished Size: Approximately 4$^1/_2$" (11.5 cm) diameter

STITCH GUIDE

Treble Crochet *(tr)* ***(Figs. 11a & b, page 60)***

SINGLE CROCHET 2 TOGETHER ***(abbreviated sc2tog)***

Pull up a loop in each of next 2 sc, YO and draw through all 3 loops on hook **(counts as one sc)**.

INSTRUCTIONS

Rnd 1 (Right side)**:** Ch 5, 23 tr in 5th ch from hook; join with slip st to top of beginning ch-5: 24 sts.

Rnd 2: Ch 1, sc in same st as joining, ch 3, (sc in next tr, ch 3) around; join with slip st to first sc: 24 ch-3 sps.

Rnd 3: Slip st in next ch-3 sp, ch 1, 2 sc in same sp and in next ch-3 sp, ch 3, (sc in next ch-3 sp, ch 3) twice, ★ 2 sc in each of next 2 ch-3 sps, ch 3, (sc in next ch-3 sp, ch 3) twice; repeat from ★ around; join with slip st to first sc: 6 4-sc groups and 18 ch-3 sps.

Rnd 4: Ch 1, skip first sc, ★ sc2tog, ch 17, skip next 3 ch-3 sps and next sc; repeat from ★ around; join with slip st to first sc: 6 loops.

Rnd 5: (Slip st, ch 1, 6 sc) in next loop, ★ † ch 6, slip st in top of last sc made ***(Fig. 1a, page 58)***, 4 sc in same loop, (ch 6, slip st, ch 7, slip st, ch 6, slip st) in top of last sc made, 4 sc in same loop, ch 6, slip st in top of last sc made †, 6 sc in same loop and in next loop; repeat from ★ 4 times **more**, then repeat from † to † once, 6 sc in same loop; join with slip st to first sc, finish off.

See Starching, page 61. Use 6-Point Blocking Pattern, page 62.

52

EASY +

Finished Size: Approximately 4" (10 cm) diameter

STITCH GUIDE

Treble Crochet *(tr)* ***(Figs. 11a & b, page 60)***

Double Treble Crochet *(dtr)* ***(Figs. 12a & b, page 60)***

BEGINNING 3-DC CLUSTER (uses one sp)

Ch 3, ★ YO, insert hook in sp indicated, YO and pull up a loop, YO and draw through 2 loops on hook; repeat from ★ once **more**, YO and draw through all 3 loops on hook.

3-DC CLUSTER (uses one sp)

★ YO, insert hook in sp indicated, YO and pull up a loop, YO and draw through 2 loops on hook; repeat from ★ 2 times **more**, YO and draw through all 4 loops on hook.

INSTRUCTIONS

Ch 6; join with slip st to form a ring.

Rnd 1 (Right side)**:** Work beginning 3-dc Cluster in ring, ★ † ch 18, slip st in 8th ch from hook **(Picot made)**, (ch 8, slip st in 8th ch from hook) twice **(2 Picots made)**, working back down spoke (series of chs and Picots just made), skip next Picot, slip st in ch at base of next Picot, ch 3, skip next 3 chs, dtr in next ch, tr in next ch, dc in next ch, hdc in next ch, sc in next ch, slip st in next 2 chs, ch 6, slip st in 4th ch from hook, ch 2 †, work 3-dc Cluster in ring; repeat from ★ 4 times **more**, then repeat from † to † once; join with slip st to top of beginning Cluster, finish off.

See Starching, page 61. Use 12-Point Blocking Pattern, page 63.

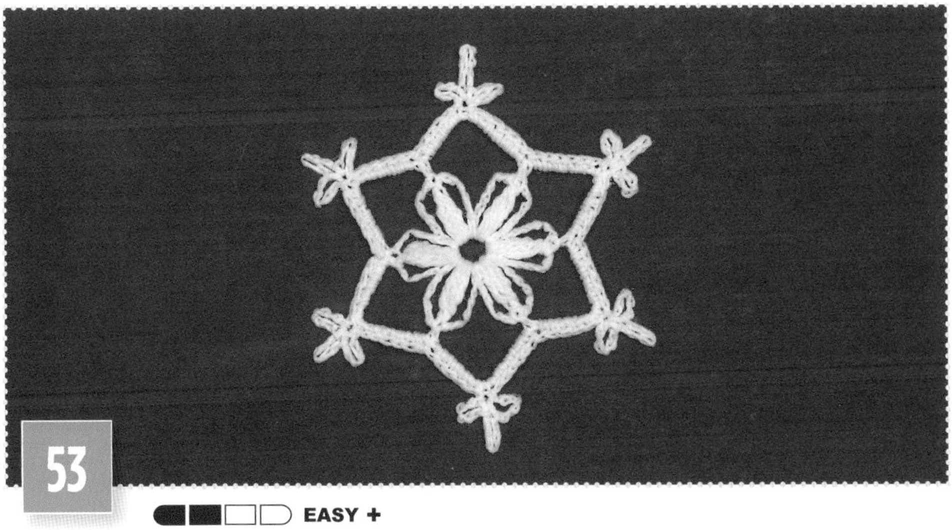

EASY +

Finished Size: Approximately 3½" (9 cm) diameter

STITCH GUIDE

BEGINNING CLUSTER (uses one sp)

Ch 4, ★ YO twice, insert hook in sp indicated, YO and pull up a loop, (YO and draw through 2 loops on hook) twice; repeat from ★ once **more**, YO and draw through all 3 loops on hook, ch 1, inserting hook from **front** to **back**, sc in top of ch-4 of Cluster ***(Fig. 1b, page 58)***.

CLUSTER (uses one sp)

★ YO twice, insert hook in sp indicated, YO and pull up a loop, (YO and draw through 2 loops on hook) twice; repeat from ★ 2 times **more**, YO and draw through all 4 loops on hook, ch 1, inserting hook from **front** to **back**, sc in sp **before** Cluster just made ***(Fig. 4, page 58)***.

INSTRUCTIONS

Ch 6; join with slip st to form a ring.

Rnd 1 (Right side)**:** Work Beginning Cluster in ring, ch 5, sc in ring, ch 5, ★ work Cluster in ring, ch 5, sc in ring, ch 5; repeat from ★ 4 times **more**; join with slip st to sc at top of Beginning Cluster: 6 Clusters.

Rnd 2: Ch 1, sc in same st as joining, ch 10, ★ sc in next sc at top of next Cluster, ch 10; repeat from ★ around; join with slip st to first sc: 6 loops.

Rnd 3: (Slip st, ch 1, 7 sc) in next loop, ★ † ch 5, slip st in top of last sc made ***(Fig. 1a, page 58)***, ch 6, (slip st, ch 5, slip st) in same sc, 6 sc in same loop †, 7 sc in next loop; repeat from ★ 4 times **more**, then repeat from † to † once; join with slip st to first sc, finish off.

See Starching, page 61. Use 6-Point Blocking Pattern, page 62.

54

EASY +

Finished Size: Approximately 3 1/2" (9 cm) diameter

STITCH GUIDE

BEGINNING CLUSTER (uses one st)
★ YO twice, insert hook in st indicated, YO and pull up a loop, (YO and draw through 2 loops on hook) twice; repeat from ★ 2 times **more**, YO and draw through all 4 loops on hook.

CLUSTER (uses one st)
★ YO twice, insert hook in st indicated, YO and pull up a loop, (YO and draw through 2 loops on hook) twice; repeat from ★ 3 times **more**, YO and draw through all 5 loops on hook.

INSTRUCTIONS

Rnd 1 (Right side)**:** Ch 5, work Beginning Cluster in 5th ch from hook, ch 6, (work Cluster in same ch, ch 6) 5 times; join with slip st to top of Beginning Cluster: 6 ch-6 sps.

Rnd 2: Slip st in next ch-6 sp, ch 1, 9 sc in same sp and in each ch-6 sp around; join with slip st to first sc: 54 sc.

Rnd 3: Ch 1, sc in same st as joining, ch 11, skip next 8 sc, ★ sc in next sc, ch 11, skip next 8 sc; repeat from ★ around; join with slip st to first sc: 6 loops.

Rnd 4: Ch 1, ★ 7 sc in next loop, ch 5, slip st in 5th ch from hook, ch 6, slip st in 6th ch from hook, ch 5, slip st in 5th ch from hook, 7 sc in same loop; repeat from ★ around; join with slip st to first sc, finish off.

See Starching, page 61. Use 6-Point Blocking Pattern, page 62.

55

EASY +

Finished Size: Approximately 4 3/4" (12 cm) diameter

STITCH GUIDE

CLUSTER (uses one sp)
★ YO twice, insert hook in sp indicated, YO and pull up a loop, (YO and draw through 2 loops on hook) twice; repeat from ★ 3 times **more**, YO and draw through all 5 loops on hook, ch 1, inserting hook from **front** to **back**, sc in sp before Cluster just made ***(Fig. 4, page 58)***

INSTRUCTIONS

Rnd 1 (Right side)**:** Ch 4, 17 dc in 4th ch from hook; join with slip st to top of beginning ch-4: 18 sts.

Rnd 2: Ch 1, sc in same st as joining, (ch 3, sc in next dc) around, ch 1, hdc in first sc to form last ch-3 sp: 18 ch-3 sps.

Rnd 3: Ch 1, sc in last ch-3 sp made, (ch 3, sc in next ch-3 sp) twice, ★ ch 5, sc in next ch-3 sp, (ch 3, sc in next ch-3 sp) twice; repeat from ★ around, ch 2, dc in first sc to form last ch-5 sp.

Rnd 4: Ch 1, sc in last ch-5 sp made, ch 11, skip next 2 ch-3 sps, ★ sc in next ch-5 sp, ch 11, skip next 2 ch-3 sps; repeat from ★ around; join with slip st to first sc: 6 loops.

Rnd 5: Slip st in next loop, ch 1, (7 sc, ch 6, 7 sc) in same loop and in each loop around; join with slip st to first sc: 84 sc and 6 ch-6 sps.

Rnd 6: Ch 1, sc in same st as joining, ★ † ch 6, work (Cluster, ch 3, Cluster) in next ch-6 sp, ch 6, slip st in 5th ch from hook, ch 1, work (Cluster, ch 3, Cluster) in same sp, ch 6, skip next 7 sc †, sc in next sc; repeat from ★ 4 times **more**, then repeat from † to † once; join with slip st to first sc, finish off.

See Starching, page 61. Use 6-Point Blocking Pattern, page 62.

56

EASY +

Finished Size: Approximately $3\frac{3}{4}$" (9.5 cm) diameter

STITCH GUIDE

Treble Crochet *(tr)* ***(Figs. 11a & b, page 60)***

CLUSTER (uses next 3 tr)

★ † YO twice, insert hook in **next** tr, YO and pull up a loop, (YO and draw through 2 loops on hook) twice †; repeat from ★ once **more**, YO twice, insert hook in **same** tr, YO and pull up a loop (6 loops on hook), (YO and draw through 2 loops on hook) twice (4 loops on hook), repeat from † to † once, YO and draw through all 5 loops on hook.

DOUBLE CLUSTER (uses next 2 ch-7 sps)

† YO twice, insert hook in **next** ch-7 sp, YO and pull up a loop, (YO and draw through 2 loops on hook) twice, ★ YO twice, insert hook in **same** ch-7 sp, YO and pull up a loop, (YO and draw through 2 loops on hook) twice; repeat from ★ 2 times **more** †, then repeat from † to † once, YO and draw through all 9 loops on hook.

INSTRUCTIONS

Ch 6; join with slip st to form a ring.

Rnd 1 (Right side)**:** Ch 4 **(counts as first tr)**, 3 tr in ring, (ch 4, 4 tr in ring) 5 times, ch 2, hdc in first tr to form last ch-4 sp: 24 tr and 6 ch-4 sps.

Rnd 2: Ch 1, sc in last ch-4 sp made, ★ † ch 7, skip next tr, work Cluster, (ch 7, slip st) twice in top of Cluster just made ***(Fig. 1b, page 58)***, ch 7 †, sc in next ch-4 sp; repeat from ★ 4 times **more**, then repeat from † to † once; join with slip st to first sc: 24 ch-7 sps.

Rnd 3: ★ Ch 11, skip next ch-7 sp, work Double Cluster, ch 6, slip st in 6th ch from hook, ch 11, skip next ch-7 sp, slip st in next sc; repeat from ★ around working last slip st in joining slip st, finish off.

See Starching, page 61. Use 6-Point Blocking Pattern, page 62.

57

EASY +

Finished Size: Approximately 4¹/₄" (11 cm) diameter

STITCH GUIDE

BEGINNING CLUSTER (uses one st or sp)

Ch 3, ★ YO, insert hook in st or sp indicated, YO and pull up a loop, YO and draw through 2 loops on hook; repeat from ★ 2 times **more**, YO and draw through all 4 loops on hook.

CLUSTER (uses one st or sp)

★ YO, insert hook in st or sp indicated, YO and pull up a loop, YO and draw through 2 loops on hook; repeat from ★ 3 times **more**, YO and draw through all 5 loops on hook.

INSTRUCTIONS

Rnd 1 (Right side)**:** Ch 5, (dc, ch 1) 11 times in 5th ch from hook; join with slip st to 4th ch of beginning ch-5: 12 ch-1 sps.

Rnd 2: (Slip st, ch 1, sc) in next ch-1 sp, ch 3, (sc in next ch-1 sp, ch 3) around; join with slip st to first sc.

Rnd 3: (Slip st, ch 1, sc) in next ch-3 sp, ch 5, sc in next ch-3 sp, ch 3, ★ sc in next ch-3 sp, ch 5, sc in next ch-3 sp, ch 3; repeat from ★ around; join with slip st to first sc.

Rnd 4: (Slip st, ch 1, 7 sc) in next ch-5 sp, sc in next ch-3 sp, (7 sc in next ch-5 sp, sc in next ch-3 sp) around; join with slip st to first sc: 48 sc.

Rnd 5: Slip st in next 2 sc, work Beginning Cluster in same st, ★ † (ch 3, work Cluster in next sc) twice, ch 5, skip next 2 sc, sc in next sc, ch 5 †, skip next 2 sc, work Cluster in next sc; repeat from ★ 4 times **more**, then repeat from † to † once, skip last 2 sts; join with slip st to top of Beginning Cluster: 18 Clusters and 24 sps.

Rnd 6: (Slip st, work Beginning Cluster) in next ch-3 sp, ★ † ch 3, work Cluster in next ch-3 sp, ch 12, skip next ch-5 sp, slip st in next sc, ch 12, skip next ch-5 sp †, work Cluster in next ch-3 sp; repeat from ★ 4 times **more**, then repeat from † to † once; join with slip st to top of Beginning Cluster: 12 Clusters, 12 loops, and 6 ch-3 sps.

Rnd 7: (Slip st, work Beginning Cluster) in next ch-3 sp, ★ † ch 15, skip next loop, working **around** next slip st ***(Fig. 2, page 58)***, slip st in sc in row **below**, ch 15, skip next loop †, work Cluster in next ch-3 sp, ch 6, slip st in 6th ch from hook, inserting hook from **front** to **back**, slip st in ch-15 loop **before** Cluster just made ***(Fig. 4, page 58)***; repeat from ★ 4 times **more**, then repeat from † to † once; join with slip st to top of Beginning Cluster, ch 6, slip st in 6th ch from hook, inserting hook from **front** to **back**, slip st in sp between last ch-15 made and first Cluster, finish off.

See Starching, page 61. Use 6-Point Blocking Pattern, page 62.

58

EASY +

Finished Size: Approximately 5" (12.5 cm) diameter

STITCH GUIDE

Treble Crochet *(tr)* ***(Figs. 11a & b, page 60)***

3-TR CLUSTER (uses one sp)

★ YO twice, insert hook in sp indicated, YO and pull up a loop, (YO and draw through 2 loops on hook) twice; repeat from ★ 2 times **more**, YO and draw through all 4 loops on hook, ch 1, inserting hook from **front** to **back**, sc in sp **before** Cluster just made ***(Fig. 4, page 58)***.

4-TR CLUSTER (uses one sp)

★ YO twice, insert hook in sp indicated, YO and pull up a loop, (YO and draw through 2 loops on hook) twice; repeat from ★ 3 times **more**, YO and draw through all 5 loops on hook, ch 1, inserting hook from **front** to **back**, sc in sp **before** Cluster just made.

SINGLE CROCHET 2 TOGETHER *(abbreviated sc2tog)*

Pull up a loop in each of next 2 ch-2 sps, YO and draw through all 3 loops on hook **(counts as one sc)**.

INSTRUCTIONS

Ch 6; join with slip st to form a ring.

Rnd 1 (Right side)**:** Ch 1, sc in ring, ch 5, work 3-tr Cluster in ring, ★ ch 5, sc in ring, ch 5, work 3-tr Cluster in ring; repeat from ★ 4 times **more**; ch 1, tr in first sc to form last ch-5 sp: 12 ch-5 sps.

Rnd 2: Ch 1, sc in last ch-5 sp made, ch 6, sc in next ch-5 sp, ★ ch 5, sc in next ch-5 sp, ch 6, sc in next ch-5 sp; repeat from ★ around, ch 2, dc in first sc to form last ch-5 sp.

Rnd 3: Ch 1, sc in last ch-5 sp made, ★ † ch 2, sc in next ch-6 sp, (ch 5, work 4-tr Cluster, ch 5, sc) twice in same sp †, ch 2, sc in next ch-5 sp; repeat from ★ 4 times **more**, then repeat from † to † once, hdc in first sc to form last ch-2 sp: 12 4-tr Clusters.

Rnd 4: Ch 1, beginning in last ch-2 sp made, sc2tog, ★ † ch 4, sc in next ch-5 sp, ch 5, sc in next ch-5 sp, ch 13, sc in next ch-5 sp, ch 5, sc in next ch-5 sp, ch 4 †, sc2tog; repeat from ★ 4 times **more**, then repeat from † to † once; join with slip st to first sc, finish off.

See Starching, page 61. Use 6-Point Blocking Pattern, page 62.

59

EASY +

Finished Size: Approximately $4^{3}/_{4}$" (12 cm) diameter

STITCH GUIDE

CLUSTER (uses one st)

★ YO, insert hook in 3rd ch from hook, YO and pull up a loop, YO and draw through 2 loops on hook; repeat from ★ once **more**, YO and draw through all 3 loops on hook.

INSTRUCTIONS

Ch 5; join with slip st to form a ring.

Rnd 1 (Right side)**:** Ch 5, (dc in ring, ch 2) 11 times; join with slip st to 3rd ch of beginning ch-5: 12 ch-2 sps.

Rnd 2: (Slip st, ch 1, sc) in next ch-2 sp, (ch 3, sc in next ch-2 sp) around, ch 1, hdc in first sc to form last ch-3 sp.

Rnd 3: Ch 1, sc in last ch-3 sp made, (ch 5, sc in next ch-3 sp) around, ch 2, dc in first sc to form last ch-5 sp.

Rnd 4: Ch 1, sc in last ch-5 sp made, ★ † ch 7, slip st in 5th ch from hook, ch 2, sc in next ch-5 sp, ch 5, work Cluster, ch 4, work Cluster, ch 5, slip st in 5th ch from hook, ch 3, work Cluster, ch 4, work Cluster, ch 2 †, sc in next ch-5 sp on Rnd 3; repeat from ★ 4 times **more**, then repeat from † to † once; join with slip st to first sc, finish off.

See Starching, page 61. Use 12-Point Blocking Pattern, page 63.

60

EASY +

Finished Size: Approximately $3^{3}/_{4}$" (9.5 cm) diameter

STITCH GUIDE

Treble Crochet *(tr)*
(Figs. 11a & b, page 60)

Double Treble Crochet *(dtr)*
(Figs. 12a & b, page 60)

CLUSTER (uses one st)

★ YO twice, insert hook in st indicated, YO and pull up a loop, (YO and draw through 2 loops on hook) twice; repeat from ★ once more, YO and draw through all 3 loops on hook.

SINGLE CROCHET 2 TOGETHER ***(abbreviated sc2tog)*** (uses one ch and one Cluster)

Pull up a loop in 4th ch of next ch-4 and in next Cluster, YO and draw through all 3 loops on hook.

INSTRUCTIONS

Rnd 1 (Right side)**:** Ch 5, (tr, ch 4, sc) in 5th ch from hook, (ch 4, work Cluster, ch 4, sc) 5 times in same ch, ch 4; join with slip st to top of beginning ch-5: 12 ch-4 sps.

Rnd 2: Ch 1, pull up a loop in same st as joining and in next tr, YO and draw through all 3 loops on hook, ★ ch 9, skip next ch-4 sp, sc2tog; repeat from ★ around, ch 4, dtr in first st to form last ch-9 sp: 6 ch-9 sps.

Rnd 3: Ch 1, sc in last ch-9 sp made, ch 12, (sc in next ch-9 sp, ch 12) around; join with slip st to first sc: 6 sc and 6 loops.

Rnd 4: Ch 1, sc in same st as joining, ★ † ch 6, sc in next loop, (ch 5, slip st in 5th ch from hook) 3 times, sc in same loop, ch 6 †, sc in next sc, ch 4, slip st in top of sc just made ***(Fig. 1a, page 58)***, sc in same sc as last sc made; repeat from ★ 4 times **more**, then repeat from † to † once, sc in same st as first sc, ch 4, slip st in top of sc just made; join with slip st to first sc, finish off.

See Starching, page 61. Use 12-Point Blocking Pattern, page 63.

61

INTERMEDIATE

Finished Size: Approximately 4 1/2" (11.5 cm) diameter

STITCH GUIDE

4-DC CLUSTER (uses next 4 dc)
★ YO, insert hook in **next** dc, YO and pull up a loop, YO and draw through 2 loops on hook; repeat from ★ 3 times **more**, YO and draw through all 5 loops on hook, ch 1, inserting hook from **front** to **back**, sc in sp **before** 4-dc Cluster just made ***(Fig. 4, page 58)***.

5-DC CLUSTER (uses next 5 dc)
★ YO, insert hook in **next** dc, YO and pull up a loop, YO and draw through 2 loops on hook; repeat from ★ 4 times **more**, YO and draw through all 6 loops on hook.

INSTRUCTIONS

Rnd 1 (Right side)**:** Ch 2, (sc, ch 3) 6 times in 2nd ch from hook; join with slip st to first sc: 6 ch-3 sps.

Rnd 2: Slip st in next ch-3 sp, ch 5 **(counts as first dc plus ch 2)**, 2 dc in same sp, (2 dc, ch 2, 2 dc) in next ch-3 sp and in each ch-3 sp around, dc in same sp as first dc; join with slip st to first dc: 24 dc and 6 ch-2 sps.

Rnd 3: Slip st in next ch-2 sp, ch 1, (sc, ch 6, sc) in same sp, ch 2, skip next 2 dc, sc in sp **before** next dc ***(Fig. 3, page 58)***, ch 2, skip next 2 dc, ★ (sc, ch 6, sc) in next ch-2 sp, ch 2, skip next 2 dc, sc in sp **before** next dc, ch 2, skip next 2 dc; repeat from ★ around; join with slip st to first sc: 18 sps.

Rnd 4: Slip st in next ch-6 sp, ch 3 **(counts as first dc)**, 5 dc in same sp, ★ † ch 6, slip st in 6th ch from hook to form a ring, leaving thread in **back**, bring hook in **front** of slip st just made to begin working on opposite side of ring, (slip st, ch 3, 5 dc, ch 1, dc) in ring, ch 3, (4 dc, ch 3, slip st) in top of last dc made, (5 dc, ch 3, slip st) in same ring, 6 dc in same ch-6 sp on Rnd 3 as previous 6-dc group, skip next 2 ch-2 sps †, 6 dc in next ch-6 sp; repeat from ★ 4 times **more**, then repeat from † to † once; join with slip st to first dc: 162 dc and 24 ch-3 sps.

Rnd 5: ★ † Ch 3, work 5-dc Cluster, ch 3, skip next ch-3 sp, work 5-dc Cluster, ch 5, sc in next ch-3 sp, ch 5, work 4-dc Cluster, ch 5, sc in next ch-3 sp, ch 5, work 5-dc Cluster, ch 3, skip next ch-3 sp, work 5-dc Cluster, ch 3, skip next dc, sc in sp **before** next dc †, slip st in next dc; repeat from ★ 4 times **more**, then repeat from † to † once; join with slip st to joining slip st, finish off.

See Starching, page 61. Use 6-Point Blocking Pattern, page 62.

62

INTERMEDIATE

Finished Size: Approximately $2\frac{3}{4}$" (7 cm) diameter

STITCH GUIDE

Treble Crochet *(tr)* ***(Figs. 11a & b, page 60)***
Double Treble Crochet *(dtr)* ***(Figs. 12a & b, page 60)***

INSTRUCTIONS

Rnd 1 (Right side)**:** Ch 6, (tr, ch 1) 11 times in 6th ch from hook; join with slip st to 5th ch of beginning ch-6: 12 ch-1 sps.

Rnd 2: Slip st in next ch-1 sp, ch 7, (dtr, ch 4, slip st) in same sp, ch 1, slip st in next ch-1 sp, ch 1, ★ (slip st, ch 4, dtr, ch 2, dtr, ch 4, slip st) in next ch-1 sp, ch 1, slip st in next ch-1 sp, ch 1; repeat from ★ around, slip st in same sp as first slip st, ch 4; join with slip st to 5th ch of beginning ch-7: 6 ch-2 sps.

Rnd 3: ★ In next ch-2 sp work (slip st, ch 4, dc, ch 5, slip st, ch 5, dc, ch 4, slip st), ch 6, sc in next ch-1 sp on Rnd 1 working **around** slip st ***(Fig. 2, page 58)***, ch 6; repeat from ★ around; join with slip st to first slip st, finish off.

See Starching, page 61. Use 6-Point Blocking Pattern, page 62.

63

INTERMEDIATE

Finished Size: Approximately $3\frac{1}{2}$" (9 cm) diameter

INSTRUCTIONS

Rnd 1 (Right side)**:** Ch 4, 11 dc in 4th ch from hook; join with slip st to top of beginning ch-4: 12 sts.

Rnd 2: ★ Ch 25, slip st in 20th ch from hook (ch-19 loop made), † leaving thread in **back**, bring hook in **front** of slip st to make a new loop on opposite side of loop just made ***(Figs. 7a & b, page 59)*** †, ch 22, slip st in 22nd ch from hook (ch-21 loop made), repeat from † to † once, ch 13, sc in top of ch-21 loop just made and in top of next ch-19 loop, ch 5, slip st in same st at base of ch-25, (slip st, ch 28, slip st) in next dc, slip st in next dc; repeat from ★ around working last slip st in joining slip st; finish off.

See Starching, page 61. Use 12-Point Blocking Pattern, page 63, twisting ch-28 loops 3 times before pinning them in place.

64

INTERMEDIATE

Finished Size: Approximately $3\frac{1}{2}$" (9 cm) diameter

INSTRUCTIONS

Ch 6; join with slip st to form a ring.

Rnd 1 (Right side)**:** Ch 1, sc in ring, (ch 5, sc in ring) 5 times, ch 2, dc in first sc to form last ch-5 sp: 6 ch-5 sps.

Rnd 2: Ch 1, sc in last ch-5 sp made, ★ † ch 8, dc in 5th ch from hook, place marker, (ch 5, dc in 5th ch from hook) twice, ch 8, slip st in 8th ch from hook, (ch 5, dc in 5th ch from hook) 3 times, slip st in marked ch to form a loop, remove marker, ch 3 †, sc in next ch-5 sp; repeat from ★ 4 times **more**, then repeat from † to † once; join with slip st to first sc, finish off.

See Starching, page 61. Use 6-Point Blocking Pattern, page 62.

65

INTERMEDIATE

Finished Size: Approximately $4\frac{1}{4}$" (11 cm) diameter

STITCH GUIDE

KNOT ST

Pull up a loop on hook to measure $\frac{1}{4}$" (7 mm), holding single strand with thumb and middle finger, ch 1 forming a sp between strand and $\frac{1}{4}$" (7 mm) loop ***(Fig. A)***, sc in sp just formed ***(Fig. B)***.

Fig. A

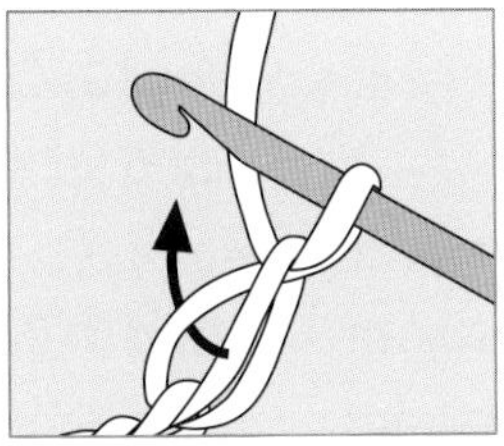

Fig. B

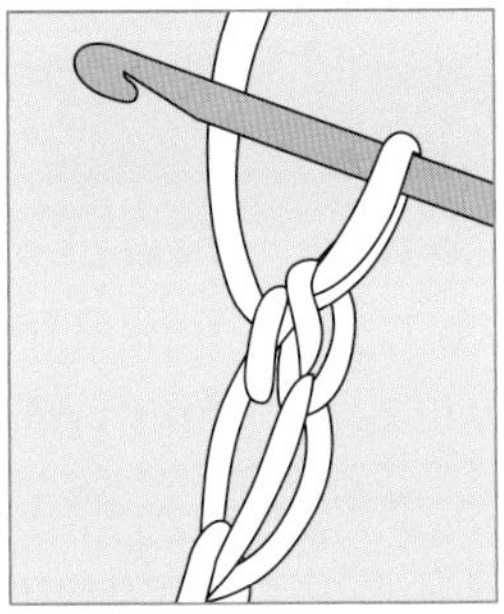

INSTRUCTIONS

Ch 5; join with slip st to form a ring.

Rnd 1 (Right side)**:** Ch 5, (dc in ring, ch 2) 11 times; join with slip st to 3rd ch of beginning ch-5: 12 ch-2 sps.

Rnd 2: (Slip st, ch 1, sc) in next ch-2 sp, ★ † ch 1, sc in next ch-2 sp, ch 16, dc in 6th ch from hook, (ch 3, skip next 2 chs, dc in next ch) twice, ch 4, skip last 4 chs †, sc in next ch-2 sp on Rnd 1; repeat from ★ 4 times **more**, then repeat from † to † once; join with slip st to first sc: 6 spokes.

Rnd 3: (Slip st, ch 1, sc) in next ch-1 sp, ★ † work 2 Knot sts, skip next ch-4 sp, sc in next ch-2 sp, work 2 Knot sts, sc in next ch-2 sp, work Knot st, (sc, work Knot st) 3 times in next ch-5 sp (at tip), (sc in next ch-3 sp, work 2 Knot sts) twice, skip next ch-4 sp †, sc in next ch-1 sp; repeat from ★ 4 times **more**, then repeat from † to † once; join with slip st to first sc, finish off.

See Starching, page 61. Use 6-Point Blocking Pattern, page 62.

66

INTERMEDIATE

Finished Size: Approximately 3¾" (9.5 cm) diameter

STITCH GUIDE

Double Treble Crochet *(dtr)* ***(Figs. 12a & b, page 60)***

Triple Treble Crochet *(tr tr)* ***(Figs. 13a & b, page 60)***

INSTRUCTIONS

Rnd 1 (Right side)**:** Ch 4, 23 dc in 4th ch from hook; join with slip st to top of beginning ch-4: 24 sts.

Rnd 2: Ch 5 **(counts as first dtr)**, 2 dtr in next dc, dtr in next dc, ch 8, skip next dc, ★ dtr in next dc, 2 dtr in next dc, dtr in next dc, ch 8, skip next dc; repeat from ★ around; join with slip st to first dtr: 24 dtr and 6 ch-8 sps.

Rnd 3: Ch 4, skip same st as joining and next 2 dtr, ★ † slip st in next dtr, ch 3, skip next ch, sc in next ch, ch 4, skip next 4 chs, sc in next ch, ch 3, skip next ch †, slip st in next dtr, ch 4, skip next 2 dtr; repeat from ★ 4 times **more**, then repeat from † to † once; join with slip st to joining slip st: 24 sps.

Rnd 4: ★ Slip st in next ch-4 sp, ch 7, slip st in 2nd ch from hook and in next 5 chs, (slip st, ch 6, 2 tr tr, ch 6, slip st) in same ch-4 sp, ch 7, slip st in 2nd ch from hook and in next 5 chs, slip st in same ch-4 sp, (slip st, ch 3, slip st) in next ch-3 sp, (slip st, ch 1, hdc, dc, ch 1, dc, hdc, ch 1, slip st) in next ch-4 sp, (slip st, ch 3, slip st) in next ch-3 sp; repeat from ★ around; join with slip st to first slip st, finish off.

See Starching, page 61. Use 12-Point Blocking Pattern, page 63.

67

INTERMEDIATE

Finished Size: Approximately 3¾" (9.5 cm) diameter

STITCH GUIDE

Treble Crochet *(tr)* ***(Figs. 11a & b, page 60)***

INSTRUCTIONS

Ch 5; join with slip st to form a ring.

Rnd 1 (Right side)**:** Ch 1, sc in ring, (ch 5, sc in ring) 5 times, ch 2, dc in first sc to form last ch-5 sp: 6 ch-5 sps.

Rnd 2: Ch 1, sc in last ch-5 sp made, ch 6, (sc in next ch-5 sp, ch 6) around; join with slip st to first sc.

Rnd 3: (Slip st, ch 1, sc) in next ch-6 sp, ★ † (ch 3, sc in same sp) twice, ch 8, tr in 5th ch from hook, [ch 5, slip st in 5th ch from hook, ch 6, slip st in 6th ch from hook, ch 5, slip st in 5th ch from hook **(3-Picot group made)**], slip st in ch at base of first Picot, ch 5, tr in 5th ch from hook, (ch 3, sc) 3 times in same ch-6 sp on Rnd 2 as previous sc †, sc in next ch-6 sp; repeat from ★ 4 times **more**, then repeat from † to † once; join with slip st to first sc, finish off.

See Starching, page 61. Use 6-Point Blocking Pattern, page 62.

68

INTERMEDIATE

Finished Size: Approximately 4" (10 cm) diameter

STITCH GUIDE

Treble Crochet *(tr)* ***(Figs. 11a & b, page 60)***

INSTRUCTIONS

Ch 6; join with slip st to form a ring.

Rnd 1 (Right side)**:** Ch 1, sc in ring, (ch 5, sc in ring) 5 times, ch 2, dc in first sc to form last ch-5 sp: 6 ch-5 sps.

Rnd 2: Ch 1, sc in last ch-5 sp made, ch 6, (sc in next ch-5 sp, ch 6) around; join with slip st to first sc.

Rnd 3: (Slip st, ch 1, sc) in next ch-6 sp, ★ † (ch 3, sc in same sp) twice, ch 8, tr in 5th ch from hook, ch 5, slip st in top of last tr made ***(Fig. 1a, page 58)***, ch 6, slip st in 6th ch from hook, ch 5, slip st in same tr as last slip st made, ch 5, tr in 5th ch from hook, (ch 3, sc) 3 times in same ch-6 sp on Rnd 2 as previous sc †, sc in next ch-6 sp; repeat from ★ 4 times **more**, then repeat from † to † once; join with slip st to first sc, finish off.

See Starching, page 61. Use 6-Point Blocking Pattern, page 62.

69

INTERMEDIATE

Finished Size: Approximately $4^{1}/_{2}$" (11.5 cm) diameter

STITCH GUIDE

Treble Crochet *(tr)* ***(Figs. 11a & b, page 60)***
Double Treble Crochet *(dtr)* ***(Figs. 12a & b, page 60)***

INSTRUCTIONS

Rnd 1 (Right side)**:** Ch 8, tr in 8th ch from hook, ch 1, (tr, ch 3, tr, ch 1) 5 times in same ch; join with slip st to 5th ch of beginning ch-8: 12 sps.

Rnd 2: Slip st in next ch-3 sp, ch 5 **(counts as first dtr)**, (3 dtr, ch 4, slip st) in same sp, ch 1, slip st in next ch-1 sp, ch 1, ★ (slip st, ch 4, 4 dtr, ch 4, slip st) in next ch-3 sp, ch 1, slip st in next ch-1 sp, ch 1; repeat from ★ around, slip st in same sp as first slip st, ch 4; join with slip st to first dtr: 24 dtr and 12 ch-4 sps.

Rnd 3: Slip st in next 2 dtr, ch 3 **(counts as first dc)**, 4 dc in same st, ★ † ch 9, dc in next ch-1 sp on Rnd 1 working **around** slip st ***(Fig. 2, page 58)***, ch 9 †, skip next ch-4 sp and next 2 dtr, 5 dc in next dtr; repeat from ★ 4 times **more**, then repeat from † to † once, skip next ch-4 sp and next 2 sts; join with slip st to first dc: 36 dc and 12 ch-9 sps.

Rnd 4: Slip st in next dc, ch 6, (dtr, ch 1, dtr) in same st, (ch 1, dtr) 3 times in next dc, ★ † (ch 6, slip st in top of last tr made) 3 times ***(Fig. 1a, page 58)***, (dtr, ch 1) 3 times in each of next 2 dc, sc in each of next 2 ch-9 sps, skip next dc †, (ch 1, dtr) 3 times in each of next 2 dc; repeat from ★ 4 times **more**, then repeat from † to † once, ch 1; join with slip st to 5th ch of beginning ch-6, finish off.

See Starching, page 61. Use 6-Point Blocking Pattern, page 62.

70

INTERMEDIATE

71

INTERMEDIATE

Finished Size: Approximately 3" (7.5 cm) diameter

STITCH GUIDE

Treble Crochet *(tr)*
(Figs. 11a & b, page 60)
Double Treble Crochet *(dtr)*
(Figs. 12a & b, page 60)
Triple Treble Crochet *(tr tr)*
(Figs. 13a & b, page 60)

INSTRUCTIONS

Ch 5; join with slip st to form a ring.

Rnd 1 (Right side)**:** Ch 1, sc in ring, (ch 3, sc in ring) 5 times, ch 1, hdc in first sc to form last ch-3 sp: 6 ch-3 sps.

Rnd 2: Ch 1, sc in last ch-3 sp made, (sc, ch 9, sc) in each of next 5 ch-3 sps, sc in same sp as first sc, ch 3, tr tr in first sc to form last ch-9 sp: 12 sc and 6 ch-9 sps.

Rnd 3: Ch 3, (tr, dtr, tr, dc, hdc, ch 2, slip st) in last ch-9 sp made, skip next 2 sc, ★ slip st in next 2 chs, ch 2, (hdc, dc, tr, dtr, tr, dc, hdc) in same ch-9 sp, ch 2, slip st in last 2 chs of same ch-9, skip next 2 sc; repeat from ★ around, slip st in next 2 chs of same ch-9 as first st, ch 2, hdc in same sp; join with slip st to top of beginning ch-3.

Rnd 4: Ch 1, sc in same st as joining, (ch 3, sc in next st) twice, ★ † ch 5, (sc in next st, ch 3) 3 times, sc in next ch-2 sp, skip next ch-2 sp, sc in next hdc †, (ch 3, sc in next st) 3 times; repeat from ★ 4 times **more**, then repeat from † to † once, ch 3; join with slip st to first sc, finish off.

See Starching, page 61. Use 6-Point Blocking Pattern, page 62.

Finished Size: Approximately 3½" (9 cm) diameter

STITCH GUIDE

Treble Crochet *(tr)*
(Figs. 11a & b, page 60)

INSTRUCTIONS

Ch 6; join with slip st to form a ring.

Rnd 1 (Right side)**:** Ch 1, (sc in ring, ch 5) 6 times; join with slip st to first sc: 6 ch-5 sps.

Rnd 2: (Slip st, ch 1, sc) in next ch-5 sp, ★ † (ch 3, sc in same sp) twice, ch 10, 2 tr in 5th ch from hook, ch 5, slip st in top of last tr made ***(Fig. 1a, page 58)***, ch 5, 2 tr in 5th ch from hook, slip st in ch at base of first 2-tr group, ch 5, sc in same ch-5 sp on Rnd 1 as previous sc, (ch 3, sc in same sp) twice †, sc in next ch-5 sp; repeat from ★ 4 times **more**, then repeat from † to † once; join with slip st to first sc, finish off.

See Starching, page 61. Use 6-Point Blocking Pattern, page 62.

INTERMEDIATE

Finished Size: Approximately 4" (10 cm) diameter

STITCH GUIDE

Treble Crochet *(tr)* ***(Figs. 11a & b, page 60)***

Double Treble Crochet *(dtr)* ***(Figs. 12a & b, page 60)***

INSTRUCTIONS

Ch 5; join with slip st to form a ring.

Rnd 1 (Right side)**:** Ch 1, sc in ring, (ch 6, sc in ring) 5 times, ch 3, dc in first sc to form last ch-6 sp: 6 ch-6 sps.

Rnd 2: Ch 1, sc in last ch-6 sp made, ★ † ch 9, dtr in 5th ch from hook, [dtr in side of last dtr made ***(Fig. 5, page 58)***] 3 times, (tr, ch 7, 2 tr) in side of last dtr made, tr in side of next 3 dtr, ch 4, slip st in same ch as first dtr, ch 4 †, sc in next ch-6 sp; repeat from ★ 4 times **more**, then repeat from † to † once; join with slip st to first sc, finish off.

See Starching, page 61. Use 6-Point Blocking Pattern, page 62.

INTERMEDIATE

Finished Size: Approximately 5" (12.5 cm) diameter

STITCH GUIDE

Treble Crochet *(tr)* ***(Figs. 11a & b, page 60)***

Double Treble Crochet *(dtr)* ***(Figs. 12a & b, page 60)***

DECREASE (uses next 3 ch-1 sps)
† YO twice, insert hook in **next** ch-1 sp, YO and pull up a loop, (YO and draw through 2 loops on hook) twice †, YO, insert hook in **next** ch-1 sp, YO and pull up a loop, YO and draw through 2 loops on hook (3 loops on hook), repeat from † to † once, YO and draw through all 4 loops on hook.

INSTRUCTIONS

Ch 5; join with slip st to form a ring.

Rnd 1 (Right side)**:** Ch 1, 12 sc in ring; join with slip st to first sc.

Rnd 2: Ch 5, dtr in same st as joining, (ch 7, 2 dtr in next sc) around, ch 3, tr in top of beginning ch-5 to form last ch-7 sp: 12 ch-7 sps.

Rnd 3: Ch 1, sc in top of last tr made ***(Fig. 1a, page 58)***, ch 11, sc in center ch of next ch-7, ★ ch 4, sc in center ch of next ch-7, ch 11, sc in center ch of next ch-7; repeat from ★ around, ch 2, hdc in first sc to form last ch-4 sp: 6 ch-4 sps and 6 loops.

Rnd 4: Ch 1, sc in last ch-4 sp made, ch 1, (dc, ch 1) 14 times in next loop, ★ sc in next ch-4 sp, ch 1, (dc, ch 1) 14 times in next loop; repeat from ★ around; join with slip st to first sc: 90 ch-1 sps.

Rnd 5: Slip st in next ch and in next dc, ch 1, ★ sc in next ch-1 sp, (ch 4, slip st in 3rd ch from hook, ch 2, skip next ch-1 sp, sc in next ch-1 sp) twice, ch 4, decrease, (ch 5, slip st in 5th ch from hook) 3 times, slip st in top of decrease, ch 4, sc in next ch-1 sp, (ch 4, slip st in 3rd ch from hook, ch 2, skip next ch-1 sp, sc in next ch-1 sp) twice, skip next 2 ch-1 sps; repeat from ★ around; join with slip st to first sc, finish off.

See Starching, page 61. Use 6-Point Blocking Pattern, page 62.

74

INTERMEDIATE

Finished Size: Approximately $3^{3}/_{4}$" (9.5 cm) diameter

STITCH GUIDE

Double Treble Crochet *(dtr)* ***(Figs. 12a & b, page 60)***

INSTRUCTIONS

Ch 6; join with slip st to form a ring.

Rnd 1 (Right side)**:** Ch 1, (sc in ring, ch 5) 6 times; join with slip st to first sc: 6 ch-5 sps.

Rnd 2: (Slip st, ch 1, sc) in next ch-5 sp, ★ † (ch 3, sc in same sp) twice, ch 8, dtr in 5th ch from hook, ch 5, slip st in 5th ch from hook, ch 6, slip st in 6th ch from hook, ch 5, slip st in 5th ch from hook, (slip st, ch 5, dtr) in top of last dtr made ***(Fig. 1a, page 58)***, ch 3, sc in same ch-5 sp on Rnd 1 as previous sc, (ch 3, sc in same sp) twice †, sc in next ch-5 sp; repeat from ★ 4 times **more**, then repeat from † to † once; join with slip st to first sc, finish off.

See Starching, page 61. Use 6-Point Blocking Pattern, page 62.

75

INTERMEDIATE

Finished Size: Approximately $5^{1}/_{2}$" (14 cm) diameter

STITCH GUIDE

Treble Crochet *(tr)* ***(Figs. 11a & b, page 60)***

Double Treble Crochet *(dtr)* ***(Figs. 12a & b, page 60)***

INSTRUCTIONS

Ch 5; join with slip st to form a ring.

Rnd 1 (Right side)**:** Ch 1, 12 sc in ring; join with slip st to first sc.

Rnd 2: Ch 8, skip next sc, ★ slip st in next sc, ch 8, skip next sc; repeat from ★ around; join with slip st to joining slip st: 6 ch-8 sps.

Rnd 3: Ch 1, (2 sc, 2 hdc, 3 dc, 2 hdc, 2 sc) in each ch-8 sp around; join with slip st to first sc: 66 sts.

Rnd 4: Ch 14 **(counts as first dtr plus ch 9)**, skip next 10 sts, ★ dtr in next sc, ch 9, skip next 10 sts; repeat from ★ around; join with slip st to first dtr: 6 tr and 6 ch-9 sps.

Rnd 5: Ch 1, (2 sc, 2 hdc, 2 dc, 2 tr, 2 dc, 2 hdc, 2 sc) in next ch-9 sp, sc in next dtr, ★ ch 6, slip st in top of last sc made ***(Fig. 1a, page 58)***, (2 sc, 2 hdc, 2 dc, 2 tr, 2 dc, 2 hdc, 2 sc) in next ch-9 sp, sc in next dtr; repeat from ★ around, ch 3, dc in top of last sc made to form last ch-6 sp: 6 ch-6 sps.

Rnd 6: Ch 6 **(counts as first tr plus ch 2)**, 2 tr in last ch-6 sp made, ch 12, ★ (2 tr, ch 2, 2 tr) in next ch-6 sp, ch 12; repeat from ★ around, tr in same sp as first tr; join with slip st to first tr: 6 ch-2 sps and 6 loops.

Rnd 7: ★ (Slip st, ch 4, 2 tr) in next ch-2 sp, **[**ch 6, slip st in 5th ch from hook, (ch 5, slip st in 5th ch from hook) twice **(3-Picot group made)]**, slip st in same ch as first Picot, ch 1, (2 tr, ch 4, slip st) in same ch-2 sp, ch 5, (2 sc, 2 hdc, 2 dc, 3 tr, 2 dc, 2 hdc, 2 sc) in next loop, ch 5; repeat from ★ around; join with slip st to first slip st, finish off.

See Starching, page 61. Use 12-Point Blocking Pattern, page 63.

76

INTERMEDIATE

Finished Size: Approximately 4½" (11.5 cm) diameter

INSTRUCTIONS

Ch 6; join with slip st to form a ring.

Rnd 1 (Right side)**:** Ch 1, sc in ring, (ch 5, sc in ring) 5 times, ch 2, dc in first sc to form last ch-5 sp: 6 ch-5 sps.

Rnd 2: Ch 1, sc in last ch-5 sp made, ch 10, slip st in 7th ch from hook to form a ring, ch 3, ★ sc in next ch-5 sp, ch 10, slip st in 7th ch from hook, ch 3; repeat from ★ around; join with slip st to first sc: 6 sc, 6 rings, and 12 ch-3 sps.

Rnd 3: ★ 3 Hdc in next ch-3 sp, (3 hdc, ch 2, 2 dc) in next ring, ch 3, **turn**; skip first dc, 2 dc in next dc, ch 3, **turn**; skip first dc, dc in next dc and in next ch, ch 3, **turn**; skip first dc, sc in next dc, ch 3, sc in next ch, ch 3, working across end of rows just made, skip next 2 chs, sc in top of next dc, ch 3, sc in top of next dc, ch 3, **turn**; (sc, ch 3) twice in each of next 4 ch-3 sps, (sc, ch 3) twice around next dc, (sc, ch 3) twice in next ch-3 sp, slip st in top of next dc, ch 2, 3 hdc in same ring on Rnd 2 and in next ch-3 sp, slip st in next sc; repeat from ★ around working last slip st in joining slip st, finish off.

See Starching, page 61. Use 6-Point Blocking Pattern, page 62.

77

INTERMEDIATE

Finished Size: Approximately 4¾" (12 cm) diameter

STITCH GUIDE

Treble Crochet *(tr)* ***(Figs. 11a & b, page 60)***

Triple Treble Crochet *(tr tr)* ***(Figs. 13a & b, page 60)***

INSTRUCTIONS

Rnd 1 (Right side)**:** Ch 5, tr in 5th ch from hook **(4 skipped chs count as first tr)**, ch 4, slip st in 3rd ch from hook, ch 1, ★ 2 tr in same ch as first tr, ch 4, slip st in 3rd ch from hook, ch 1; repeat from ★ 4 times **more**; join with slip st to first tr: 12 tr.

Rnd 2: Slip st in next tr, ch 4 **(counts as first tr)**, tr in same st, ch 10, skip next tr, ★ 2 tr in next tr, ch 10, skip next tr; repeat from ★ around; join with slip st to first tr: 12 tr and 6 loops.

Rnd 3: ★ Slip st in next tr, (ch 4, slip st in 3rd ch from hook) 5 times, ch 8, slip st in 7th ch from hook, (ch 4, slip st in 3rd ch from hook) 5 times, ch 1, (slip st, ch 6, tr tr) in same tr, hdc in next loop, (tr tr, ch 6, slip st) in next tr; repeat from ★ around working last group in joining slip st, finish off.

See Starching, page 61. Use 12-Point Blocking Pattern, page 63.

INTERMEDIATE

Finished Size: Approximately 3¹/₂" (9 cm) diameter

STITCH GUIDE

Double Treble Crochet *(dtr)*
(Figs. 12a & b, page 60)

INSTRUCTIONS

Ch 6; join with slip st to form a ring.

Rnd 1 (Right side)**:** Ch 1, 12 sc in ring; join with slip st to first sc.

Rnd 2: ★ Ch 12, (dtr, ch 6, slip st) in 6th ch from hook, slip st in next 6 chs and in sc at base of ch-12, slip st in next 2 sc; repeat from ★ around working last slip st in joining slip st: 6 Spokes.

Rnd 3: ★ Ch 7, sc in ch at base of next dtr, (ch 3, sc) 4 times in next ch-6 sp, ch 4, (sc, ch 3) 4 times in next ch-6 sp, sc in ch at base of dtr, ch 7, skip next 6 slip sts, slip st in next 2 slip sts (between Spokes), ch 3, slip st in 3rd ch from hook and in next slip st; repeat from ★ around working last slip st in joining slip st; finish off.

See Starching, page 61. Use 6-Point Blocking Pattern, page 62.

INTERMEDIATE

Finished Size: Approximately 3¹/₂" (9 cm) diameter

INSTRUCTIONS

Ch 6; join with slip st to form a ring.

Rnd 1 (Right side)**:** Ch 3 **(counts as first dc, now and throughout)**, (dc, ch 3, slip st) in ring, (ch 3, 2 dc, ch 3, slip st) 5 times in ring, ch 3; join with slip st to first dc: 12 dc and 12 ch-3 sps.

Rnd 2: Slip st in next dc, ch 11, skip next 2 ch-3 sps and next dc, ★ dc in next dc, ch 8, skip next 2 ch-3 sps and next st; repeat from ★ around; join with slip st to 3rd ch of beginning ch-11: 6 ch-8 sps.

Rnd 3: (Slip st, ch 3, 4 dc) in next ch-8 sp, 2 dc in side of last dc made ***(Fig. 5, page 58)***, 4 dc in same ch-8 sp, ★ 5 dc in next ch-8 sp, 2 dc in side of last dc made, 4 dc in same ch-8 sp; repeat from ★ around; join with slip st to first dc: 66 dc.

Rnd 4: Ch 3, dc in next dc, (dc, ch 4, slip st) in next dc, ★ † ch 1, slip st in next 4 dc, ch 21, slip st in 12th ch from hook, ch 9, slip st in same dc at base of ch-21, ch 1, slip st in next 3 dc, (slip st, ch 4, dc) in next dc †, dc in next 3 dc, ch 1, **turn**; slip st in first 2 dc, ch 3, dc in next 2 dc, ch 5, **turn**; skip first 3 dc, slip st in next 2 slip sts, ch 4, slip st in dc at base of same dc; repeat from ★ 4 times **more**, then repeat from † to † once, join with slip st to first dc, slip st in next dc, ch 3, **turn**; skip first dc, dc in next 2 dc, ch 5, **turn**; skip first 3 dc, slip st in next dc; finish off.

See Starching, page 61. Use 12-Point Blocking Pattern, page 63.

80

INTERMEDIATE

Finished Size: Approximately $4^{1}/_{2}$" (11.5 cm) diameter

STITCH GUIDE

Treble Crochet *(tr)* ***(Figs. 11a & b, page 60)***

INSTRUCTIONS

Rnd 1 (Right side)**:** Ch 5, 17 tr in 5th ch from hook; join with slip st to top of beginning ch-5: 18 sts.

Rnd 2: Ch 4 **(counts as first tr, now and throughout)**, tr in same st as joining, ch 6, skip next 2 tr, ★ 3 tr in next tr, ch 6, skip next 2 tr; repeat from ★ around, tr in same st as first tr; join with slip st to first tr: 18 tr and 6 ch-6 sps.

Rnd 3: Ch 4, tr in same st as joining, ★ † ch 2, 2 tr in next tr, ch 4, sc in next ch-6 sp, ch 4, slip st in top of last sc made ***(Fig. 1a, page 58)*** **(Picot made)**, sc in same ch-6 sp, ch 4, skip next tr †, 2 tr in next tr; repeat from ★ 4 times **more**, then repeat from † to † once; join with slip st to first tr: 6 Picots and 18 sps.

Rnd 4: Slip st in next tr and in next ch-2 sp, ch 4, 2 tr in same sp, ★ † (ch 7, slip st in 4th ch from hook) 3 times, ch 3, 3 tr in same ch-2 sp as last tr made, ch 4, slip st in top of last tr made, ch 4, sc in next ch-4 sp, ch 6, slip st in 4th ch from hook, ch 2, skip next Picot, sc in next ch-4 sp, ch 8, slip st in 4th ch from hook †, 3 tr in next ch-2 sp; repeat from ★ 4 times **more**, then repeat from † to † once; join with slip st to first tr, finish off.

See Starching, page 61. Use 12-Point Blocking Pattern, page 63.

81

INTERMEDIATE

Finished Size: Approximately 5" (12.5 cm) diameter

INSTRUCTIONS

Ch 6; join with slip st to form a ring.

Rnd 1 (Right side)**:** Ch 2 **(counts as first hdc)**, 17 hdc in ring; join with slip st to first hdc: 18 hdc.

Rnd 2: Ch 1, sc in same st, ★ † ch 20, slip st in 12th ch from hook to form a ring, leaving thread in **back**, bring hook in **front** of slip st just made to begin working on opposite side of ring ***(Figs. 7a & b, page 59)***, (slip st, ch 2, 7 dc, ch 2, 4 sc) in ring, ch 5, slip st in 5th ch from hook, ch 6, slip st in 6th ch from hook, ch 5, slip st in 5th ch from hook, (4 sc, ch 2, 7 dc, ch 2, slip st) in same ring, slip st in ch at base of ring, ch 8, skip next 2 hdc †, sc in next hdc; repeat from ★ 4 times **more**, then repeat from † to † once; join with slip st to first sc, finish off.

See Starching, page 61. Use 6-Point Blocking Pattern, page 62.

82

INTERMEDIATE

Finished Size: Approximately $3^{1}/_{4}$" (8.5 cm) diameter

INSTRUCTIONS

Rnd 1 (Right side)**:** Ch 18, ★ † slip st in 11th ch from hook to form a ring, leaving thread in **back**, bring hook in **front** of slip st just made to begin working on opposite side of ring ***(Figs. 7a & b, page 59)***, (ch 5, slip st in 3rd ch from hook) 7 times, ch 2, slip st in ch at base of ring, slip st in next 6 chs of spoke and in first ch of beginning ch-18 †, ch 17; repeat from ★ 4 times **more**, then repeat from † to † once; finish off.

See Starching, page 61. Use 6-Point Blocking Pattern, page 62.

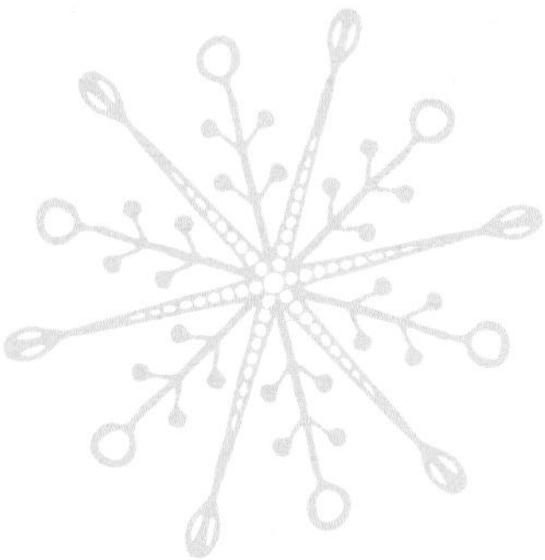

83

INTERMEDIATE

Finished Size: Approximately $4^{3}/_{4}$" (12 cm) diameter

STITCH GUIDE

Treble Crochet *(tr)* ***(Figs. 11a & b, page 60)***

INSTRUCTIONS

Ch 6; join with slip st to form a ring.

Rnd 1 (Right side)**:** Ch 3 **(counts as first dc)**, 17 dc in ring; join with slip st to first dc: 18 dc.

Rnd 2: Ch 1, sc in same st as joining, ★ ch 7, skip next 2 dc, sc in next dc; repeat from ★ around to last 2 dc, ch 3, skip last 2 dc, tr in first sc to form last ch-7 sp: 6 ch-7 sps.

Rnd 3: Ch 1, sc in last ch-7 sp made, ★ † ch 17, slip st in 12th ch from hook to form a ring, ch 1, leaving thread in **back**, bring hook in **front** of slip st just made to begin working on opposite side of ring ***(Figs. 7a & b, page 59)***, (sc, hdc, 5 dc, 7 tr, 5 dc, hdc, sc) in ring, slip st in ch in **front** of slip st, ch 5 †, sc in next ch-7 sp; repeat from ★ 4 times **more**, then repeat from † to † once; join with slip st to first sc: 6 rings and 12 ch-5 sps.

Rnd 4: (Slip st, ch 1, sc) in next ch-5 sp, ★ † (ch 3, sc in same sp) 3 times, skip next sc, slip st in next hdc, ch 3, (skip next st, sc in next st, ch 3) 8 times, skip next dc, slip st in next hdc, skip next sc †, [sc in next ch-5 sp, (ch 3, sc in same sp) 3 times] twice; repeat from ★ 4 times **more**, then repeat from † to † once, sc in next ch-5 sp, (ch 3, sc in same sp) 3 times; join with slip st to first sc, finish off.

See Starching, page 61. Use 6-Point Blocking Pattern, page 62.

84

INTERMEDIATE

Finished Size: Approximately 4 1/2" (11.5 cm) diameter

INSTRUCTIONS

Rnd 1 (Right side)**:** Ch 4, 17 dc in 4th ch from hook; join with slip st to top of beginning ch-4: 18 sts.

Rnd 2: ★ Ch 21, slip st in 12th ch from hook to form a ring, † leaving thread in **back**, bring hook in **front** of slip st just made to begin working on opposite side of ring ***(Figs. 7a & b, page 59)***, ch 6, sc in ring †, (ch 6, slip st in 6th ch from hook) 3 times **(3-Picot group made)**, (slip st, ch 12, slip st) in ch at base of first Picot, repeat from † to † once, ch 9, slip st in dc at base of same spoke, sc in next dc, ch 21, slip st in 6th ch from hook, ch 15, sc in next dc, slip st in next dc; repeat from ★ around working last slip st in joining slip st; finish off.

See Starching, page 61. Use 12-Point Blocking Pattern, page 63.

85

INTERMEDIATE

Finished Size: Approximately 5 3/4" (14.5 cm) diameter

INSTRUCTIONS

Ch 5; join with slip st to form a ring.

Rnd 1 (Right side)**:** Ch 1, sc in ring, (ch 3, sc in ring) 5 times, ch 1, hdc in first sc to form last ch-3 sp: 6 ch-3 sps.

Rnd 2: Ch 3 **(counts as first dc)**, 2 dc in last ch-3 sp made, (3 dc, ch 2, 3 dc) in next ch-3 sp and in each ch-3 sp around, 3 dc in same sp as first dc, ch 1, sc in first dc to form last ch-2 sp: 36 dc and 6 ch-2 sps.

Rnd 3: Ch 5, 3 dc in last ch-2 sp made, ch 3, skip next 6 dc, ★ (3 dc, ch 2, 3 dc) in next ch-2 sp, ch 3, skip next 6 dc; repeat from ★ around, 2 dc in same sp as first dc; join with slip st to 3rd ch of beginning ch-5: 12 sps.

Rnd 4: Slip st in next ch-2 sp, ch 1, (sc, ch 6, sc) in same sp, ch 5, sc in next ch-3 sp, ch 5, ★ (sc, ch 6, sc) in next ch-2 sp, ch 5, sc in next ch-3 sp, ch 5; repeat from ★ around; join with slip st to first sc: 18 sps.

Rnd 5: ★ (Slip st, ch 3, 5 dc, ch 1, dc) in next ch-6 sp, ch 6, slip st in top of last dc made to form a ring ***(Fig. 1a, page 58)***, ch 1, leaving thread in **back**, bring hook in **front** of slip st just made to begin working on opposite side of ring ***(Figs. 7a & b, page 59)***, (slip st, ch 3, 5 dc, ch 1, dc) in ring, ch 3, (4 dc, ch 3, slip st) in top of last dc made, (5 dc, ch 3, slip st) in same ring and in next ch-6 sp, ch 3, (sc in next ch-5 sp, ch 3) twice; repeat from ★ around; join with slip st to first slip st, finish off.

See Starching, page 61. Use 6-Point Blocking Pattern, page 62.

Finished Size: Approximately 4" (10 cm) diameter

INSTRUCTIONS

Ch 5; join with slip st to form a ring.

Rnd 1 (Right side)**:** Ch 7, dc in ring, (ch 4, dc in ring) 10 times, ch 2, hdc in 3rd ch of beginning ch-7 to form last ch-4 sp: 12 ch-4 sps.

Rnd 2: Ch 1, sc in last ch-4 sp made, ★ † ch 15, slip st in top of last sc made to form a ring *(Fig. 1a, page 58)*, leaving thread in **back**, bring hook in **front** of slip st just made to begin working on opposite side of ring *(Figs. 7a & b, page 59)*, (ch 3, sc in ring) 10 times, sc in same sc as slip st at base of ring †, (ch 4, sc in next ch-4 sp) twice; repeat from ★ 4 times **more**, then repeat from † to † once, ch 4, sc in next ch-4 sp, ch 2, hdc in first sc to form last ch-4 sp: 72 sps.

Rnd 3: Ch 1, sc in last ch-4 sp made and in next ch-3 sp, ★ † (ch 3, sc in next ch-3 sp) 9 times, sc in next ch-4 sp, ch 3 †, sc in next ch-4 sp and in next ch-3 sp; repeat from ★ 4 times **more**, then repeat from † to † once; join with slip st to first sc, finish off.

See Starching, page 61. Use 6-Point Blocking Pattern, page 62.

Finished Size: Approximately $4^3/_4$" (12 cm) diameter

INSTRUCTIONS

Ch 5; join with slip st to form a ring.

Rnd 1 (Right side)**:** Ch 8, dc in ring, (ch 5, dc in ring) 4 times, ch 2, dc in 3rd ch of beginning ch-8 to form last ch-5 sp: 6 ch-5 sps.

Rnd 2: Ch 1, sc in last ch-5 sp made, ch 7, (sc in next ch-5 sp, ch 7) around; join with slip st to first sc.

Rnd 3: Ch 1, sc in same st as joining, ★ † ch 15, slip st in 15th ch from hook to form a ring, leaving thread in **back**, bring hook in **front** of slip st just made to begin working on opposite side of ring *(Figs. 7a & b, page 59)*, ch 7, (dc in ring, ch 3, slip st in top of last dc made) 5 times *(Fig. 1a, page 58)*, ch 5, (dc in ring, ch 3, slip st in top of last dc made) 5 times, ch 7, slip st in ch at base of ring, sc in same sc on Rnd 2 as previous sc, ch 4, sc in next ch-7 sp, ch 4, slip st in top of last sc made, sc in same ch-7 sp, ch 4 †, sc in next sc; repeat from ★ 4 times **more**, then repeat from † to † once; join with slip st to first sc, finish off.

See Starching, page 61. Use 12-Point Blocking Pattern, page 63.

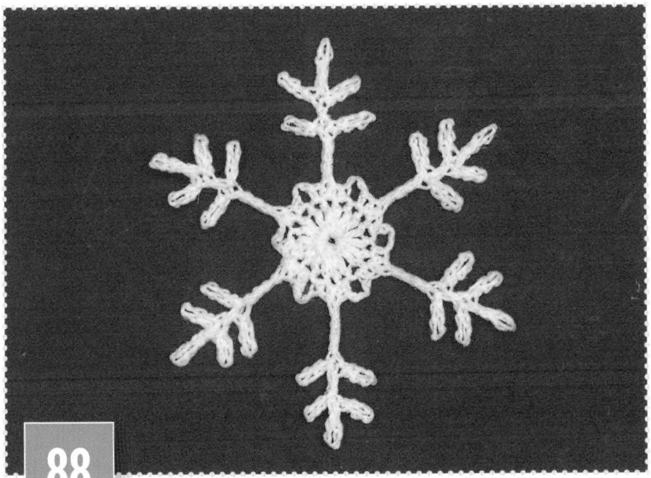

INTERMEDIATE

Finished Size: Approximately 3¹/₄" (8.5 cm) diameter

INSTRUCTIONS

Rnd 1 (Right side)**:** Ch 4, 17 dc in 4th ch from hook; join with slip st to top of beginning ch-4: 18 sts.

Rnd 2: Ch 1, sc in same st as joining, ★ † ch 11, slip st in 7th ch from hook **(Picot made)**, ch 7, slip st in 6th ch from hook, ch 6, slip st in 5th ch from hook **(top Picot)** and in next ch, ch 6, slip st in 6th ch from hook; working back down spoke (series of chs and Picots just made), skip top Picot and slip st in ch at base of next Picot and in next ch *(Fig. 6, page 59)*, ch 7, slip st in 7th ch from hook, slip st in ch at base of next Picot and in next 4 chs, sc in same st as sc at bottom of spoke and in next dc, ch 3 †, sc in next 2 dc; repeat from ★ 4 times **more**, then repeat from † to † once, sc in last dc; join with slip st to first sc, finish off.

See Starching, page 61. Use 6-Point Blocking Pattern, page 62.

INTERMEDIATE

Finished Size: Approximately 3¹/₄" (8.5 cm) diameter

INSTRUCTIONS

Rnd 1 (Right side)**:** Ch 3, 11 hdc in 3rd ch from hook; join with slip st to top of beginning ch-3: 12 sts.

Note: Loop a short piece of thread around any stitch to mark Rnd 1 as **right** side.

Rnd 2: ★ Ch 11, slip st in 6th ch from hook **(Picot made)**, ch 6, slip st in 6th ch from hook and in ch at base of first Picot, slip st in next 5 chs and in same st at base of spoke, slip st in next 2 hdc; repeat from ★ around working last slip st in joining slip st; finish off: 12 Picots.

Rnd 3: With **right** side facing, join thread with slip st in st between 2 Picots on any spoke; ★ ch 7, slip st in 6th ch from hook, ch 5, slip st in 5th ch from hook, ch 4, slip st in 4th ch from hook **(top Picot made)**, ch 5, slip st in 5th ch from hook, working back down spoke (series of chs and Picots just made), skip top Picot, slip st in ch at base of next Picot *(Fig. 6, page 59)*, ch 6, slip st in 6th ch from hook and in ch at base of next Picot, slip st in next ch, ch 19, slip st in st between next 2 Picots on next spoke; repeat from ★ around working last slip st in joining slip st; finish off.

See Starching, page 61. Use 6-Point Blocking Pattern, page 62.

90

INTERMEDIATE

Finished Size: Approximately 5¼" (13.5 cm) diameter

INSTRUCTIONS

Ch 6; join with slip st to form a ring.

Rnd 1 (Right side)**:** Ch 5, (dc in ring, ch 2) 11 times; join with slip st to 3rd ch of beginning ch-5: 12 ch-2 sps.

Rnd 2: (Slip st, ch 1, sc) in next ch-2 sp, ★ † ch 7, slip st in 3rd ch from hook **(Picot made)**, (ch 5, slip st in 3rd ch from hook) 6 times; working back down spoke (series of chs and Picots just made), skip next 2 chs, slip st in ch at base of next Picot *(Fig. 6, page 59)*, (ch 5, slip st in 3rd ch from hook and in ch at base of next Picot) 5 times, ch 4, sc in same ch-2 sp on Rnd 1 as previous sc, ch 3, (sc, ch 3) twice in next ch-2 sp †, sc in next ch-2 sp; repeat from ★ 4 times **more**, then repeat from † to † once; join with slip st to first sc, finish off.

See Starching, page 61. Use 6-Point Blocking Pattern, page 62.

91

INTERMEDIATE

Finished Size: Approximately 4" (10 cm) diameter

STITCH GUIDE

Treble Crochet *(tr)* *(Figs. 11a & b, page 60)*

INSTRUCTIONS

Rnd 1 (Right side)**:** Ch 4, 11 dc in 4th ch from hook; join with slip st to top of beginning ch-4: 12 sts.

Rnd 2: Ch 1, sc in same st as joining, ★ ch 3, skip next dc, sc in next dc; repeat from ★ around to last dc, ch 1, skip last dc, hdc in first sc to form last ch-3 sp: 6 ch-3 sps.

Rnd 3: Ch 4 **(counts as first tr)**, tr in last ch-3 sp made, ch 8, (2 tr in next ch-3 sp, ch 8) around; join with slip st to first tr: 12 tr and 6 ch-8 sps.

Rnd 4: ★ Slip st in next tr, ch 8, slip st in 5th ch from hook **(Picot made)**, ch 6, slip st in 6th ch from hook, ch 3, slip st in 3rd ch from hook, ch 9, slip st in 9th ch from hook **(top Picot made)**, ch 3, slip st in 3rd ch from hook, working back down spoke (series of chs and Picots just made), skip top Picot, slip st in ch at base of next Picot *(Fig. 6, page 59)*, ch 6, slip st in 6th ch from hook and in ch at base of next Picot, ch 5, slip st in 5th ch from hook and in ch at base of next Picot, slip st in next 3 chs, (slip st, ch 4, tr) in same tr at base of spoke, sc in next ch-8 sp, (tr, ch 4, slip st) in next tr; repeat from ★ around; join with slip st to first slip st, finish off.

See Starching, page 61. Use 12-Point Blocking Pattern, page 63.

92

INTERMEDIATE

Finished Size: Approximately 3" (7.5 cm) diameter

INSTRUCTIONS

Rnd 1 (Right side)**:** Ch 7, ★ † slip st in 3rd ch from hook **(Picot made)**, ch 11, slip st in 2nd ch from hook and in next 5 chs **(needle made)**, [ch 7, slip st in 4th ch from hook, (ch 4, slip st in 4th ch from hook) twice **(3-Picot group made)**], working back down spoke (series of chs and Picots just made), slip st in ch at base of first Picot of group and in next 3 chs ***(Fig. 6, page 59)***, ch 7, slip st in 2nd ch from hook and in next 5 chs, slip st in ch at base of next needle, ch 4, skip next 4 chs, slip st in ch at base of next Picot, ch 3, slip st in 3rd ch from hook and in ch at base of same Picot, slip st in next 3 chs and in first ch of beginning ch-7 †, ch 6; repeat from ★ 4 times **more**, then repeat from † to † once; finish off.

See Starching, page 61. Use 6-Point Blocking Pattern, page 62.

93

INTERMEDIATE

Finished Size: Approximately 3½" (9 cm) diameter

STITCH GUIDE

Treble Crochet *(tr)* ***(Figs. 11a & b, page 60)***

INSTRUCTIONS

Rnd 1 (Right side)**:** Ch 3, 11 hdc in 3rd ch from hook; join with slip st to top of beginning ch-3: 12 sts.

Rnd 2: Ch 1, (hdc, dc, tr) in same st as joining, (tr, dc, hdc) in next hdc, ★ (hdc, dc, tr) in next hdc, (tr, dc, hdc) in next hdc; repeat from ★ around; join with slip st to first hdc: 36 sts.

Rnd 3: Ch 1, sc in same st as joining, ch 11, skip next 5 sts, ★ sc in next hdc, ch 11, skip next 5 sts; repeat from ★ around; join with slip st to first sc: 6 loops.

Rnd 4: ★ Ch 5, slip st in 3rd ch from hook **(Picot made)**, ch 7, slip st in 7th ch from hook, ch 9, slip st in 9th ch from hook **(top Picot made)**, ch 7, slip st in 7th ch from hook, working back down spoke (series of chs and Picots just made), skip top Picot, slip st in ch at base of next Picot ***(Fig. 6, page 59)***, ch 3, slip st in 3rd ch from hook and in ch at base of next Picot, slip st in next 2 chs and in same sc at base of spoke, ch 1, in next loop work (hdc, 2 dc, hdc, ch 2, sc, ch 2, hdc, 2 dc, hdc), ch 1, slip st in next sc; repeat from ★ around working last slip st in joining slip st; finish off.

See Starching, page 61. Use 12-Point Blocking Pattern, page 63.

94

INTERMEDIATE

Finished Size: Approximately 4" (10 cm) diameter

STITCH GUIDE

Treble Crochet *(tr)* *(Figs. 11a & b, page 60)*

INSTRUCTIONS

Rnd 1 (Right side)**:** Ch 4, 11 dc in 4th ch from hook; join with slip st to top of beginning ch-4: 12 sts.

Rnd 2: Ch 1, (sc, ch 4, sc) in same st as joining, ★ ch 3, skip next dc, (sc, ch 4, sc) in next dc; repeat from ★ around to last dc, ch 1, skip last dc, hdc in first sc to form last ch-3 sp: 12 sps.

Rnd 3: Ch 4 **(counts as first tr)**, tr in last ch-3 sp made, ch 8, slip st in 3rd ch from hook **(Picot made)**, ch 5, skip next ch-4 sp, ★ 2 tr in next ch-3 sp, ch 8, slip st in 3rd ch from hook, ch 5, skip next ch-4 sp; repeat from ★ around; join with slip st to first tr: 12 tr and 12 ch-5 sps.

Rnd 4: Ch 3, slip st in same st as joining, ★ † ch 8, slip st in 6th ch from hook, ch 7, slip st in 6th ch from hook, ch 4, slip st in 3rd ch from hook, ch 7, slip st in 7th ch from hook **(top Picot made)**, ch 3, slip st in 3rd ch from hook, working back down spoke (series of chs and Picots just made), skip top Picot, slip st in ch at base of next Picot *(Fig. 6, page 59)*, (ch 7, slip st in 6th ch from hook and in ch at base of next Picot) twice, slip st in next 2 chs, (slip st, ch 3, slip st) in next tr, slip st in next ch-5 sp, ch 5, slip st in 3rd ch from hook, (ch 4, slip st in 3rd ch from hook) 4 times, ch 2, slip st in next ch-5 sp †, (slip st, ch 3, slip st) in next tr; repeat from ★ 4 times **more**, then repeat from † to † once; join with slip st to joining slip st, finish off.

See Starching, page 61. Use 12-Point Blocking Pattern, page 63, pinning Picots on Rnd 3 toward the center.

95

INTERMEDIATE

Finished Size: Approximately 4" (10 cm) diameter

STITCH GUIDE

Treble Crochet *(tr)* *(Figs. 11a & b, page 60)*

INSTRUCTIONS

Rnd 1 (Right side)**:** Ch 14, ★ † slip st in 5th ch from hook **(Picot made)**, ch 7, slip st in 5th ch from hook and in next 2 chs, ch 16, slip st in 10th ch from hook, ch 12, slip st in 5th ch from hook and in next 2 chs, ch 1, slip st in ch at base of first Picot, ch 5, slip st in 5th ch from hook and in ch at base of same Picot, ch 4 †, tr in 1st ch of beginning ch-14, ch 9, slip st in 3rd ch from hook, ch 6, slip st in top of last tr made *(Fig. 1a, page 58)*, ch 9; repeat from ★ 4 times **more**, then repeat from † to † once; join with slip st to 5th ch of beginning ch-14, ch 9, slip st in 3rd ch from hook, ch 6, slip st in same ch of beginning ch-14; finish off.

See Starching, page 61. Use 12-Point Blocking Pattern, page 63.

96

INTERMEDIATE

97

INTERMEDIATE

Finished Size: Approximately 4½" (11.5 cm) diameter

INSTRUCTIONS

Rnd 1 (Right side)**:** Ch 2, 6 sc in 2nd ch from hook; join with slip st to first sc.

Rnd 2: ★ Ch 3, dc in 3rd ch from hook, ch 8, slip st in 8th ch from hook **(Picot made)**, ch 11, slip st in 7th ch from hook and in next 2 chs **(needle made)**, ch 11, slip st in 8th ch from hook **(Picot made)**, ch 13, slip st in 11th ch from hook and in next 2 chs, ch 8, slip st in 8th ch from hook, working back down spoke (series of chs and Picots just made), slip st in ch at base of next Picot and in next 3 chs *(Fig. 6, page 59)*, ch 9, slip st in 7th ch from hook and in next 2 chs, slip st in ch at base of next needle and in next 2 chs, ch 8, slip st in 8th ch from hook and in ch at base of next Picot, ch 3, dc in 3rd ch from hook, slip st in ch at base of spoke and in next sc; repeat from ★ around working last slip st in same sc as first spoke; finish off.

See Starching, page 61. Use 6-Point Blocking Pattern, page 62.

Finished Size: Approximately 4¾" (12 cm) diameter

STITCH GUIDE

Double Treble Crochet *(dtr)* *(Figs. 12a & b, page 60)*

INSTRUCTIONS

Ch 6; join with slip st to form a ring.

Rnd 1 (Right side)**:** Ch 3 **(counts as first dc)**, 2 dc in ring, ch 3, (3 dc in ring, ch 3) 5 times; join with slip st to first dc: 18 dc and 6 ch-3 sps.

Rnd 2: ★ Slip st in next dc, ch 6, slip st in 2nd ch from hook and in next ch **(Picot made)**, ch 7, slip st in 5th ch from hook and in next 2 chs **(top Picot made)**, ch 3, slip st in 2nd ch from hook and in next ch, working back down spoke (series of chs and Picots just made), skip top Picot, slip st in ch at base of next Picot and in next 3 chs *(Fig. 6, page 59)*, slip st in dc at base of spoke, ch 1, skip next dc, (slip st, ch 4, dtr) in next ch-3 sp, ch 6, slip st in 2nd ch from hook and in next 2 chs, ch 7, slip st in 2nd ch from hook and in next ch, ch 6, slip st in 2nd ch from hook and in next 2 chs **(top Picot made)**, ch 5, slip st in 2nd ch from hook and in next ch, ch 1, working back down spoke, skip top Picot, next Picot, and next ch, slip st in next 3 chs, ch 4, slip st in 2nd ch from hook and in next 2 chs, slip st in ch at base of next Picot and in next 2 chs, slip st in top of same dtr at base of spoke, ch 4, slip st in same ch-3 sp as dtr, ch 1, skip next st; repeat from ★ around; join with slip st to first slip st, finish off.

See Starching, page 61. Use 12-Point Blocking Pattern, page 63.

98

INTERMEDIATE

Finished Size: Approximately 5" (12.5 cm) diameter

STITCH GUIDE

Treble Crochet *(tr)* ***(Figs. 11a & b, page 60)***

Double Treble Crochet *(dtr)* ***(Figs. 12a & b, page 60)***

INSTRUCTIONS

Rnd 1 (Right side)**:** Ch 4, 11 dc in 4th ch from hook; join with slip st to top of beginning ch-4: 12 sts.

Rnd 2: Ch 1, sc in same st as joining, ch 1, sc in next dc, ch 3, ★ sc in next dc, ch 1, sc in next dc, ch 3; repeat from ★ around; join with slip st to first sc: 12 sps.

Rnd 3: Slip st in next ch-1 sp, ch 4 **(counts as first tr)**, tr in same sp, ch 9, skip next ch-3 sp, ★ 2 tr in next ch-1 sp, ch 9, skip next ch-3 sp; repeat from ★ around; join with slip st to first tr: 12 tr and 6 ch-9 sps.

Rnd 4: Slip st in next tr, ★ † ch 8, slip st in 5th ch from hook **(Picot made)**, ch 7, slip st in 6th ch from hook, ch 4, slip st in 3rd ch from hook, ch 10, slip st in 10th ch from hook **(top Picot made)**, ch 3, slip st in 3rd ch from hook, working back down spoke (series of chs and Picots just made), skip top Picot, slip st in ch at base of next Picot *(Fig. 6, page 59)*, ch 7, slip st in 6th ch from hook and in ch at base of next Picot, ch 6, slip st in 5th ch from hook and in ch at base of next Picot, slip st in next 3 chs, (slip st, ch 5, dtr) in tr at base of spoke, hdc in next ch-9 sp †, skip next tr, (dtr, ch 5, slip st) in next tr; repeat from ★ 4 times **more**, then repeat from † to † once, skip next st, (dtr, ch 5, slip st) in tr at base of first spoke; finish off.

See Starching, page 61. Use 12-Point Blocking Pattern, page 63.

99

INTERMEDIATE

Finished Size: Approximately 4½" (11.5 cm) diameter

STITCH GUIDE

Treble Crochet *(tr)* ***(Figs. 11a & b, page 60)***

INSTRUCTIONS

Ch 6; join with slip st to form a ring.

Rnd 1 (Right side)**:** ★ Ch 4, 2 tr in ring, ch 4, **turn**; skip first tr, slip st in next tr and in next ch, (ch 11, slip st in 2nd ch from hook and in next 5 chs) twice **(1st and 2nd needles made)**, ch 7, slip st in 2nd ch from hook and in next 5 chs, ch 6, slip st in 2nd ch from hook and in next 4 chs, (ch 7, slip st in 2nd ch from hook and in next 5 chs) twice, slip st in ch at base of 2nd needle, ch 11, slip st in 2nd ch from hook and in next 5 chs, ch 4, with **right** side facing, skip next ch-4, slip st in tr at base of ch-4, ch 4, slip st in ring; repeat from ★ 5 times **more**; finish off.

See Starching, page 61. Use 12-Point Blocking Pattern, page 63.

GENERAL INSTRUCTIONS

ABBREVIATIONS

ch(s)	chain(s)
cm	centimeters
dc	double crochet(s)
dtr	double treble crochet(s)
hdc	half double crochet(s)
mm	millimeters
qtr	quadruple treble crochet(s)
Rnd(s)	Round(s)
sc	single crochet(s)
sc2tog	single crochet 2 together
sp(s)	space(s)
st(s)	stitch(es)
tr	treble crochet(s)
tr tr	triple treble crochet(s)
YO	yarn over

SYMBOLS & TERMS

★ — work instructions following ★ as many **more** times as indicated in addition to the first time.

† to † — work all instructions from first † to second † **as many** times as specified.

( ) or **[ ]** — work enclosed instructions **as many** times as specified by the number immediately following **or** work all enclosed instructions in the stitch or space indicated **or** contains explanatory remarks.

colon (:) — the number(s) given after a colon at the end of a round denote(s) the number of stitches and/or spaces you should have on that round.

STEEL CROCHET HOOKS	
Metric mm	U.S.
3.5	00
3.25	0
2.75	1
2.25	2
2.1	3
2	4
1.9	5
1.8	6
1.65	7
1.5	8
1.4	9
1.3	10
1.1	11
1	12
.85	13
.75	14

Yarn Weight Symbol & Names	LACE 0	SUPER FINE 1	FINE 2	LIGHT 3	MEDIUM 4	BULKY 5	SUPER BULKY 6
Type of Yarns in Category	Fingering, 10-count crochet thread	Sock, Fingering Baby	Sport, Baby	DK, Light Worsted	Worsted, Afghan, Aran	Chunky, Craft, Rug	Bulky, Roving
Crochet Gauge* Ranges in Single Crochet to 4" (10 cm)	32-42 double crochets**	21-32 sts	16-20 sts	12-17 sts	11-14 sts	8-11 sts	5-9 sts
Advised Hook Size Range	Steel*** 6,7,8 Regular hook B-1	B-1 to E-4	E-4 to 7	7 to I-9	I-9 to K-10.5	K-10.5 to M-13	M-13 and larger

*GUIDELINES ONLY: The chart above reflects the most commonly used gauges and hook sizes for specific yarn categories.

** Lace weight yarns are usually crocheted on larger-size hooks to create lacy openwork patterns. Accordingly, a gauge range is difficult to determine. Always follow the gauge stated in your pattern.

*** Steel crochet hooks are sized differently from regular hooks–the higher the number the smaller the hook, which is the reverse of regular hook sizing.

CROCHET TERMINOLOGY		
UNITED STATES		INTERNATIONAL
slip stitch (slip st)	=	single crochet (sc)
single crochet (sc)	=	double crochet (dc)
half double crochet (hdc)	=	half treble crochet (htr)
double crochet (dc)	=	treble crochet(tr)
treble crochet (tr)	=	double treble crochet (dtr)
double treble crochet (dtr)	=	triple treble crochet (ttr)
triple treble crochet (tr tr)	=	quadruple treble crochet (qtr)
skip	=	miss

BEGINNER	Projects for first-time crocheters using basic stitches. Minimal shaping.
EASY	Projects using yarn with basic stitches, repetitive stitch patterns, simple color changes, and simple shaping and finishing.
INTERMEDIATE	Projects using a variety of techniques, such as basic lace patterns or color patterns, mid-level shaping and finishing.
EXPERIENCED	Projects with intricate stitch patterns, techniques and dimension, such as non-repeating patterns, multi-color techniques, fine threads, small hooks, detailed shaping and refined finishing.

WORKING IN TOP OF A STITCH

When instructed to work in top of a stitch, work in loop(s) indicated by arrow *(Figs. 1a & b)*.

Fig. 1a

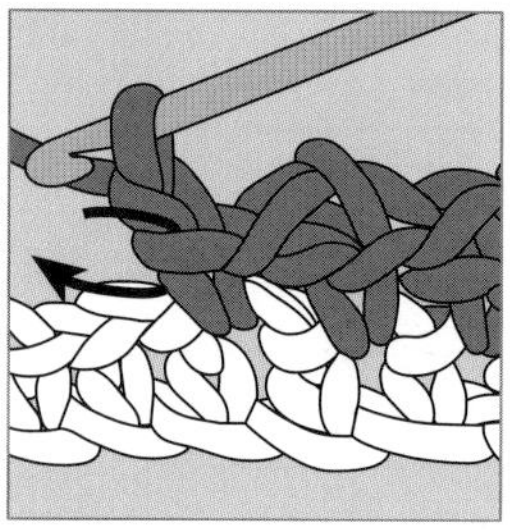

Fig. 1b

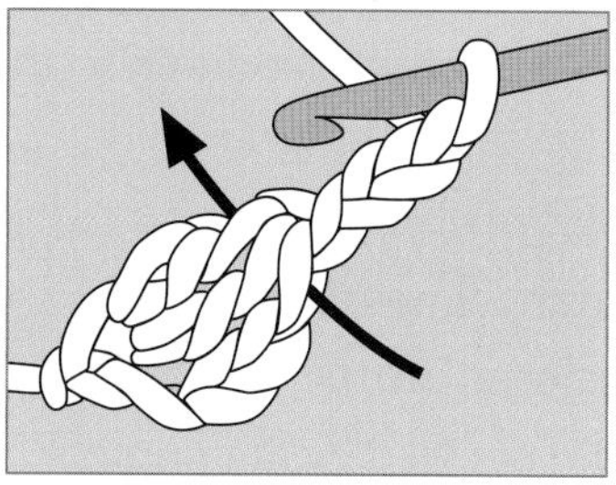

WORKING AROUND A STITCH

Work in stitch or space indicated, inserting hook in direction of arrow *(Fig. 2)*.

Fig. 2

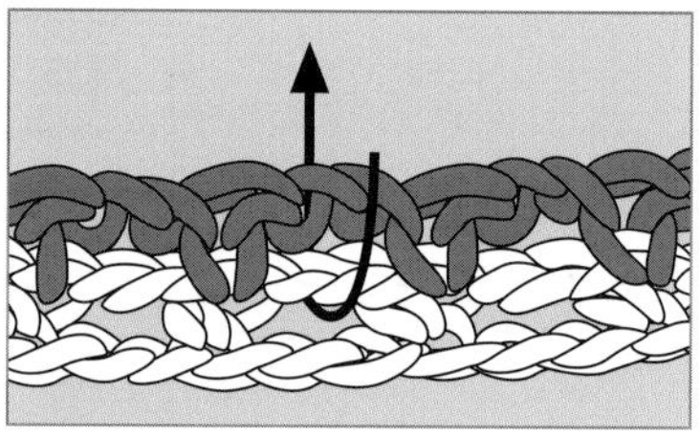

WORKING IN A SPACE BEFORE A STITCH

When instructed to work in space before a stitch, insert hook in space indicated by arrow *(Fig. 3)*.

Fig. 3

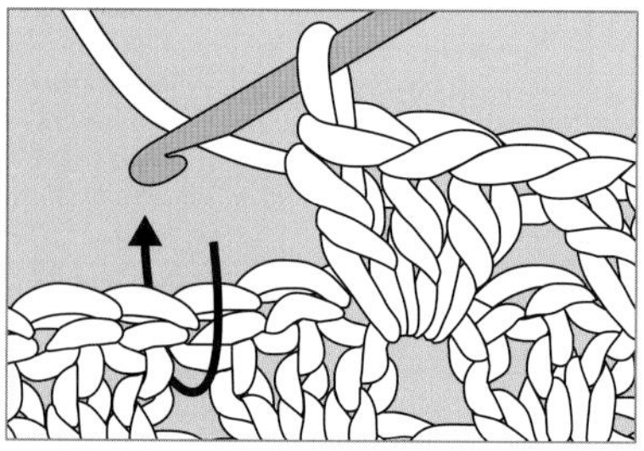

WORKING IN A SPACE BEFORE CLUSTER JUST MADE

When instructed to work in a space **before** Cluster just made, insert hook from **front** to **back** in space indicated by arrow *(Fig. 4)*.

Fig. 4

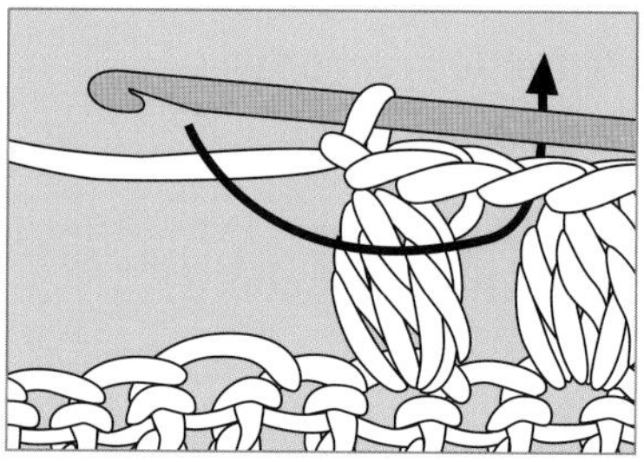

WORKING IN SIDE OF LAST STITCH MADE

When instructed to work in side of last stitch made, insert hook as indicated by arrow *(Fig. 5)*.

Fig. 5

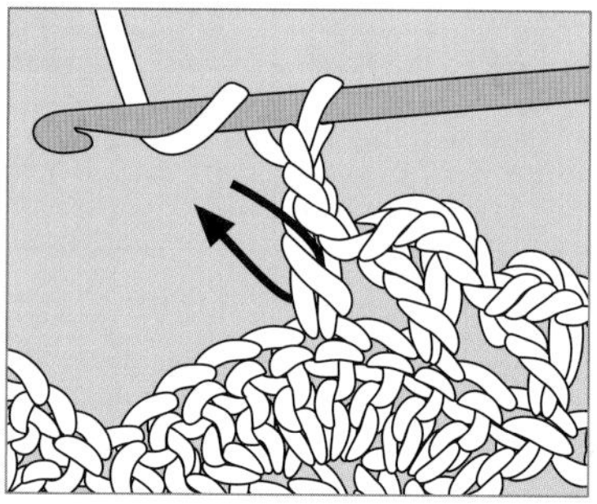

SPOKES

A Picot is formed by working a slip st in the beginning of a short chain. The chain can be any length. A spoke is formed by working a series of Picots of the same or different sizes with extra chains between the Picots.

To work back down the chain to form a mirror image on the opposite side, work Picots and slip sts in chains or in base of Picots *(Fig. 6)* as instructed.

Fig. 6

WORKING ON OPPOSITE SIDE OF RING

Leaving thread in **back** of snowflake, bring hook in **front** of slip st just made to begin working on opposite side of ring *(Figs. 7a & b)*.

Fig. 7a

Fig. 7b

Note: These Figs. are shown in yarn to make it easier to see.

BASIC STITCHES

SINGLE CROCHET *(abbreviated sc)*

Insert hook in st or sp indicated, YO and pull up a loop, (YO and draw through both loops on hook *(Fig. 8)*.

Fig. 8

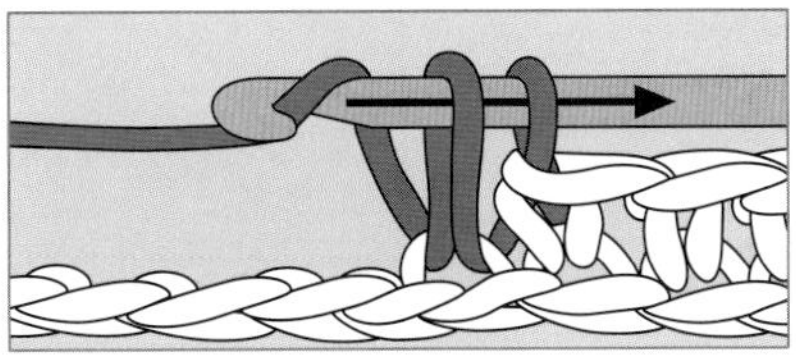

HALF DOUBLE CROCHET *(abbreviated hdc)*

YO, insert hook in st or sp indicated, YO and pull up a loop, (YO and draw through all 3 loops on hook *(Fig. 9)*.

Fig. 9

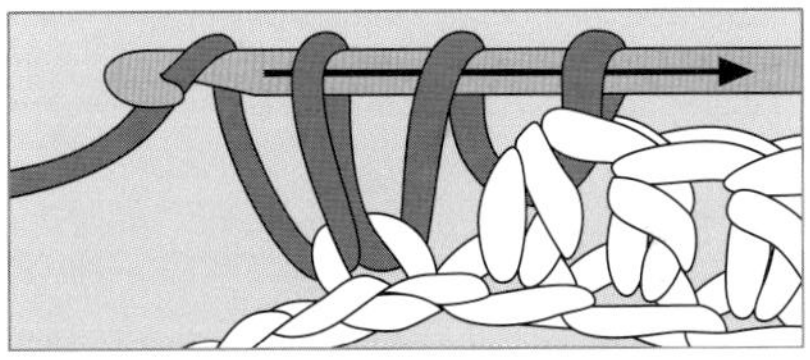

DOUBLE CROCHET *(abbreviated dc)*

YO, insert hook in st or sp indicated, YO and pull up a loop (3 loops on hook) *(Fig. 10a)*, (YO and draw through 2 loops on hook) twice *(Fig. 10b)*.

Fig. 10a

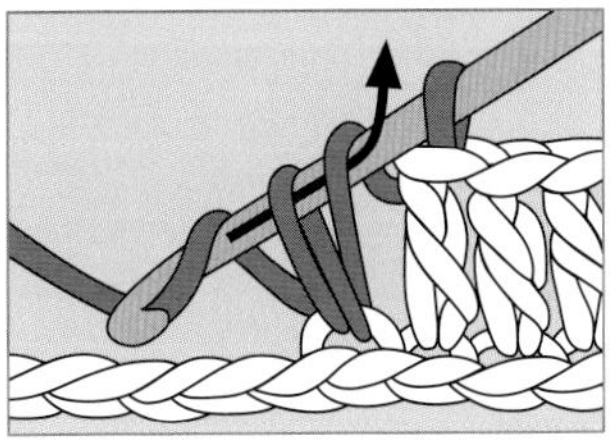

Fig. 10b

TREBLE CROCHET *(abbreviated tr)*

YO twice, insert hook in st or sp indicated, YO and pull up a loop (4 loops on hook) ***(Fig. 11a)***, (YO and draw through 2 loops on hook) 3 times ***(Fig. 11b)***.

Fig. 11a

Fig. 11b

DOUBLE TREBLE CROCHET
(abbreviated dtr)

YO 3 times, insert hook in st or sp indicated, YO and pull up a loop (5 loops on hook) ***(Fig. 12a)***, (YO and draw through 2 loops on hook) 4 times ***(Fig.12b)***.

Fig. 12a

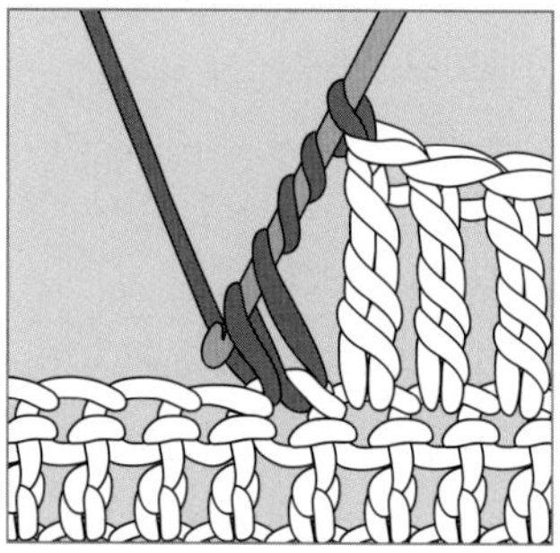

Fig. 12b

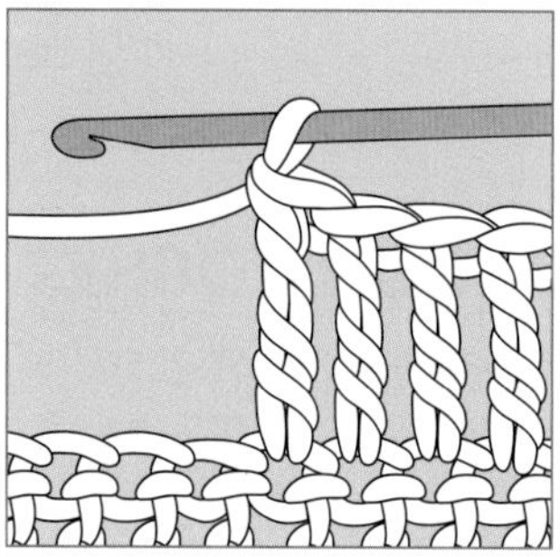

TRIPLE TREBLE CROCHET
(abbreviated tr tr)

YO 4 times, insert hook in st or sp indicated, YO and pull up a loop (6 loops on hook) ***(Fig. 13a)***, (YO and draw through 2 loops on hook) 5 times ***(Fig. 13b)***.

Fig. 13a

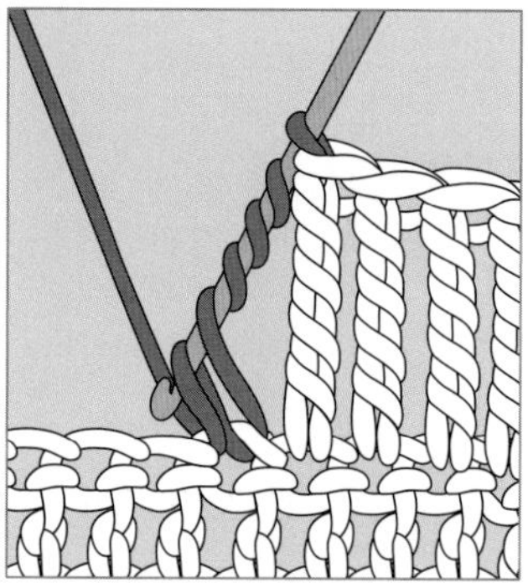

Fig. 13b

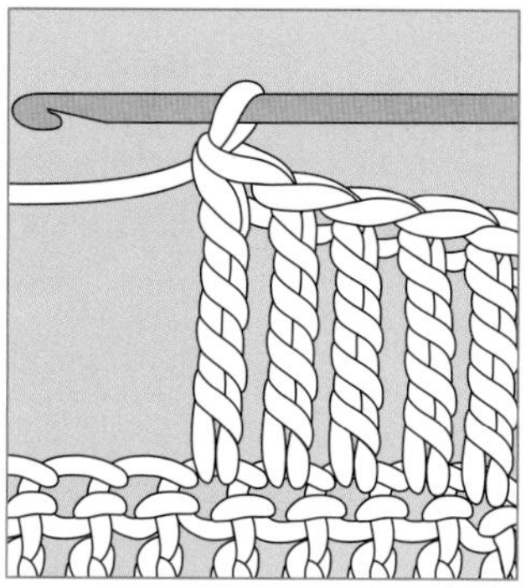

QUADRUPLE TREBLE CROCHET
(abbreviated qtr)

YO 5 times, insert hook in st or sp indicated, YO and pull up a loop (7 loops on hook) ***(Fig. 14a)***, (YO and draw through 2 loops on hook) 6 times ***(Fig. 14b)***.

Fig. 14a

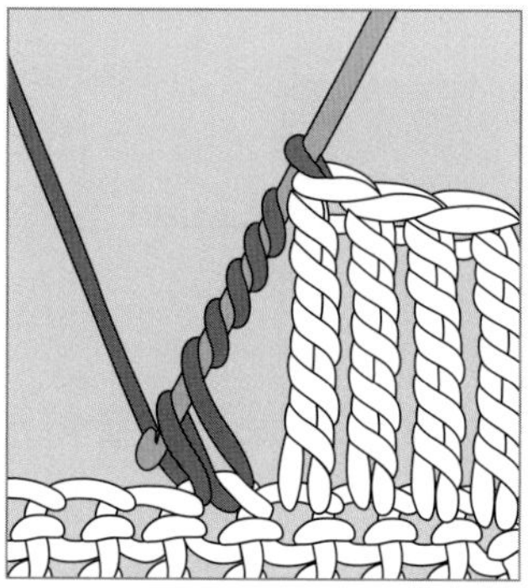

Fig. 14b

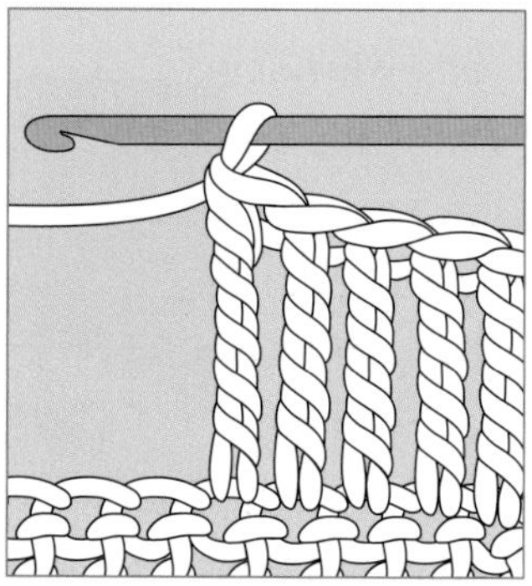

STARCHING

Snowflakes require a stiffening process to achieve the desired effect. You can change the look of many of the snowflakes as you shape them during the starching process. See Snowflakes #38 and #45 below.

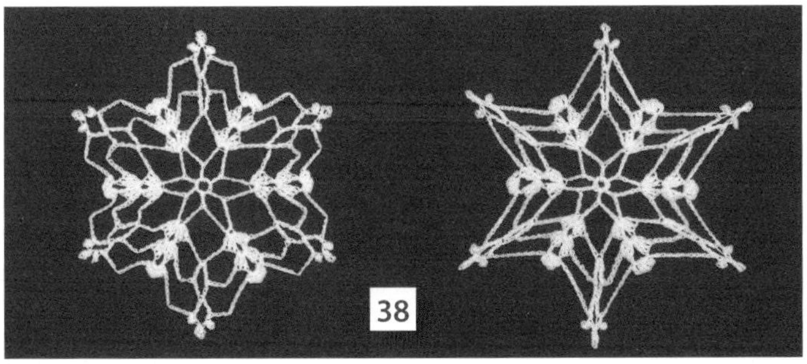

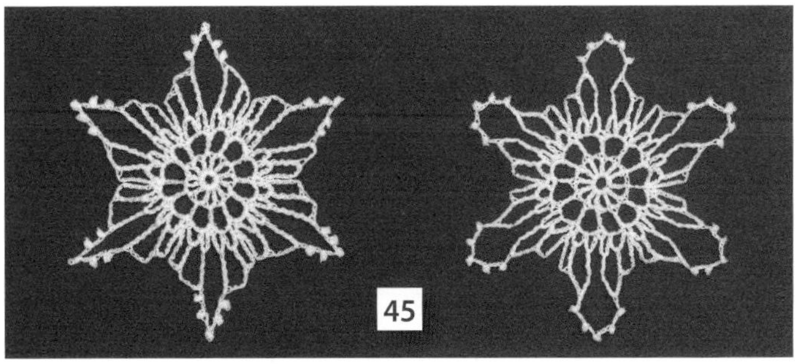

Read all of the following instructions before beginning.

1. Wash Snowflakes using a mild detergent and warm water. Rinse thoroughly. Roll piece in a clean terry towel and gently press out the excess moisture. Lay piece flat and allow to dry completely.

2. Pour fabric stiffener in a resealable plastic bag. Do not dilute stiffener. ***Note:*** This method is permanent and will not wash out.

3. Immerse dry Snowflake in fabric stiffener, remove air, and seal the bag. Work stiffener thoroughly into the piece. Let soak for several hours or overnight.

4. With tracing paper and a waterproof marking pen, trace blocking pattern needed, pages 62 and 63, as many times as necessary. Place pattern(s) on an ironing board or blocking board and cover with plastic wrap.

5. Remove Snowflakes from stiffener and squeeze gently to remove as much excess stiffener as possible. Blot with a paper towel several times to remove excess from holes.

6. With **right** side facing, spread a Snowflake over a blocking pattern and choose the mark on the long line that best fits the length of the spokes. Pin the tip of each spoke to the same mark throughout, then pin all of the components within the spoke. Use the short lines if needed to align the components between the spokes. Use the marks on the short lines in the same manner.

7. Allow to dry **completely**.

8. Make a loop hanger using translucent nylon thread.

STARCHING TIPS

1. A good blocking board can make pinning easier. Ceiling board (tile) is inexpensive, works very well, and is available at home improvement, lumber, and hardware stores.

2. Stainless steel pins with balls on the ends will be easier to use and will help prevent sore fingertips. Fabric stiffener will permanently damage pins. You may want to set these pins aside for use in future starching projects.

3. Three pins can be used for the larger Picots to open them up.

4. Fabric stiffener can be returned to the bottle and re-used if it has not been contaminated with particles or dye. Clip one corner of the bag, then squeeze the bag, forcing the stiffener to flow into the bottle.

5. Use a hard bristle toothbrush to remove excess dried fabric stiffener from finished Snowflakes.

6. After stiffener has dried completely, an acrylic spray can be used to protect the piece from heat and humidity.

BLOCKING PATTERNS

6 POINT

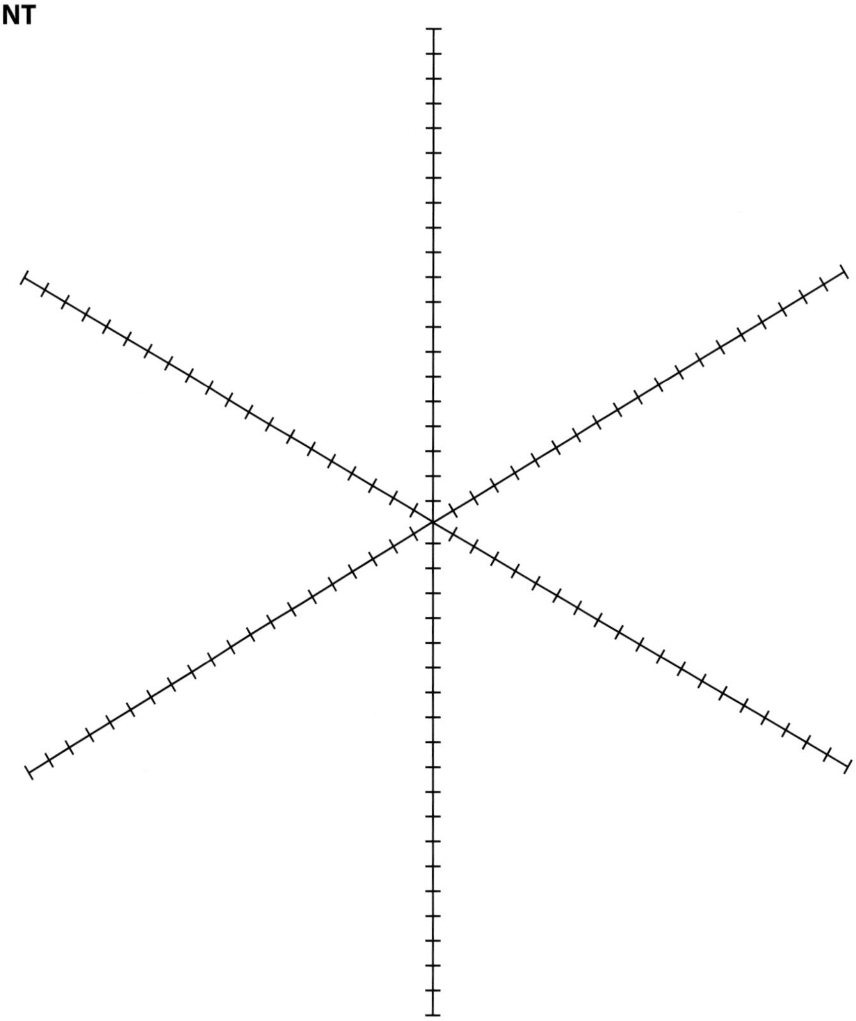

12 POINT

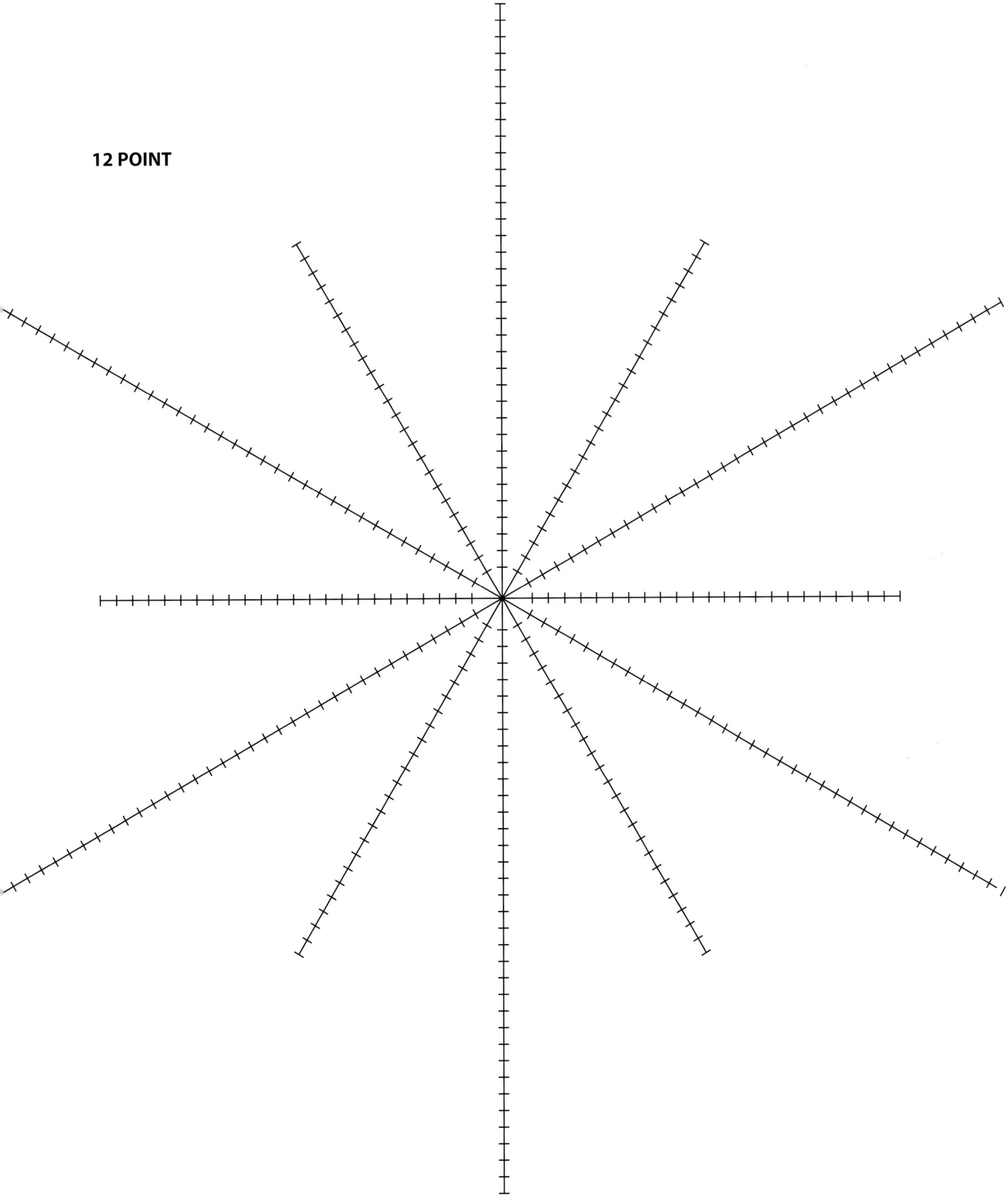

THREAD INFORMATION

The photographed snowflakes were made using a bedspread weight cotton thread (size 10). Any of the following brands may be used with good results:

Aunt Lydia's® Bamboo Crochet Thread
Aunt Lydia's® Classic Crochet
Bernat® Handicrafter® Crochet Cotton
DMC Cebelia
DMC Traditions
J. & P. Coats® Knit-Cro-Sheen®
South Maid®

MEET TERESE POEHNELT

Living in Wisconsin, Terese Poehnelt has seen her share of snowflakes. But the ones she likes best are crocheted. The inspiration for this book of 99 snowflakes came when she was a vendor at a craft fair and a young woman remarked that she was collecting snowflakes – "each one different, each one unique."

That intrigued Terese, and she started experimenting. Her resulting creations range in size from 2" to 6" across. The number of points radiating out vary from six to twelve or more, with some tips softly rounded and others sharp or edged with frills. She even designed two that can give a different look from the same pattern, just by changing how you stretch it during the starching stage. Another pattern has three variations created by adding one more round of stitches each time. What they all have in common is that they are each different and unique.

Along with snowflakes, Terese's favorite crochet projects are doilies and ornaments. Seeing a picture of crocheted doilies in a farming magazine was one of two events that sparked her initial interest in teaching herself to crochet. The other spark came from seeing an afghan as it was being crocheted by a boyfriend's mother.

Terese also enjoys other needle arts, especially when she gets to combine several skills, such as embroidery, cross stitch, and crochet, all in one piece. She also has tried her hand at tatting, but she says she has yet to succeed: "My knots end up on the wrong thread!" Considering the perseverance Terese exhibited in designing these 99 snowflakes, success is just around the corner!